CHRISTOF WIECHERT

Solving the Riddle of th
The art of the child study

CHRISTOF WIECHERT

Solving the Riddle of the Child

The art of the child study

VERLAG AM GOETHEANUM

www.vamg.ch

Translated by Matthew Barton

Cover-Design: Wolfram Schildt, Berlin, by using a drawing
by Hans Dieter Appenrodt
Copyright 2014 by Verlag am Goetheanum, CH–4143 Dornach
All rights reserved
Typesetting: Höpcke, Hamburg
Printing and binding: Druckhaus Nomos, Sinzheim
ISBN 978-3-7235-1527-3

CONTENTS

PREFACE

In our present, dramatic times, fraught with many conflicts, contradictions and upheavals, the way children are brought up and educated is of eminent importance for the future. 93 years after the first independent Waldorf school was founded, questions about the intrinsic nature of Waldorf pedagogy are still surfacing both in current public debate and internally in the Waldorf movement, in ongoing review. Such questioning includes concerns about how Steiner education today can ensure that its methodologies are not static traditions but are formed anew, and developed further, through its engagement with current educational realities. In the light of this question, it is worth looking back to see how the origins of Waldorf education relate to its present developments.

In September 1919, when he founded the Waldorf School, Rudolf Steiner's awareness of contemporary needs led him to draw on the findings of anthroposophy to formulate a set of tools – rather than any fixed curriculum – for creating a new, innovative educational praxis. As their primary task, the first teachers in Stuttgart learned to artistically shape their teaching material so that the potential capacities in each and every child could be perceived and nurtured.

Fast forward to May 2012: a Class 4 has just been singing and clapping the rhythmic variations of a round, with skill and visible enjoyment. But now the atmosphere changes all at once as five children come to the front of the class. A girl singing away boisterously a moment ago, now speaks her personal morning verse, received from her teacher with her last annual school report; and does so with such gravity and grace that for a moment she appears older and more mature than she is. Like a prefiguring of future life her words sound through the room: *'Encompassed in radiant blue, the eagle soars aloft ...'*

To usher forth such developmental powers, which emerge only within the child himself, requires a stance from the teacher that is both attentive and creatively engaged. Waldorf pedagogy becomes a living art of the present moment in the actual, tangible encounter between teacher and pupil. Our interior life and outer surroundings meet in one accord in our heartbeat; and in the same way, in the 'pedagogical moment', inward and outward development meet and merge: the child's experience with the teacher's awareness, and his alert perception with his capacity for action and initiative.

In devoting this book entirely to the art of studying and observing children, Christof Wiechert at the same time enquires into the heart organ of the Waldorf school itself, and brings it into focus as a place of confluence and encounter. It becomes apparent that the inner, latent capacity of mind or psyche of all involved can come to full fruition here. Likewise, there is no tangible external occurrence in the daily life of a school which cannot be perceived and evaluated in a down-to-earth yet loving awareness of the child. But how exactly can a 'perceiving community' of school colleagues form and develop as a shared organ of subtler, more sensitive perception of child development, with a view to better understanding and supporting it?

It is indicative of the qualities of this book that such questions, here founded on a wealth of actual accounts and descriptions, are taken up and addressed from many angles and at many levels. After engaging with the origins and development of the child study, for instance, the author goes on to illumine current questions about this theme arising within school faculties. Problems in handling the child study are discussed in such a frank and detailed way that the author's train of thought invariably leads us on to new ideas, approaches and practical possibilities. His many years of experience as a class-teacher and director of the Pedagogical Section of the School of Spiritual Science enable him to home in on sensitive aspects of the child study: How does the teaching faculty need to prepare for this work? What qualities of thinking are required to discern important strands amidst a multiplicity of phenomena? How must the ground be prepared in order for pedagogical insights and intuitions to take root?

Wherever descriptions of outward realities lead us into a consideration of soul and spiritual dimensions, the author finds incisive and often vivid words to convey them. His immediacy and originality of language allows us to share in his experiences, and stimulates our own activity and engagement in diverse ways.

This quality of stimulus for action culminates in later chapters in the author's especially rich elaboration of the third and concluding stage of a child study: What help can our teaching provide in any situation? Anthroposophic understanding of the human being here penetrates the Waldorf curriculum in so resonant a way, in terms of living polarities, that a sense of eager anticipation can arise: the thought of bringing new awareness to the question of how to help and support a child in practical ways when we next undertake a child study in the teachers' faculty.

The perspectives presented here on the art of the child study become symphonic in scope: alongside the depth, detail and precision of proposed measures, and their imaginative but always eminently practical variations, this book elicits above all our own active engagement and further endeavour. Thus real joy of discovery arises in us: the impulse to gain insight into a child's intrinsic being through our combined perception, as colleagues, of all aspects of his nature.

Claus-Peter Roeh

The coherence of the whole

Seeing what is truly great, and validating it, is only one half of insight; we overreach ourselves if we merely sing its praises, for it stands there whole, transfigured and unmatched before us. Really applying it to our human existence is wisdom and a lofty achievement. But our task of tasks is to transform the minuscule into the great, the inconspicuous into the luminous; to present a grain of dust in a way that shows it resting in the whole; to know that we cannot see it without seeing all the stars too, and the deeper context of the heavens, to which it so intimately belongs.

Rainer Maria Rilke

1. FOREWORD: THE INDIVIDUAL AND THE COMMUNITY

This book concerns studies of children and adolescents,* of the kind Rudolf Steiner suggested for the teachers' meetings of the first Waldorf school in Stuttgart. On frequent occasions he himself undertook such studies with the faculty.

In Holland, over many years, we have developed the practical skills needed to perceive the growing child so that we can decipher the riddle of his nature and get the educational process moving (again). Going back to the origins of this discipline, and reviving it, we have called it the 'art of child study'. The stimulus to do this came from the executive council of the Dutch Anthroposophical Society.

The council's treasurer, Hans Lap, first urged the then Society chairman, Ate Koopmans (born 2.2.1931, died 4.1.2002) to work with the Society's vice-chairman on re-enlivening child studies by drawing on karma exercises devised by Rudolf Steiner which he, Koopmans, had used in his courses. This gave rise to the way of

---

* Translator's note: For ease of expression these are referred to throughout as 'child studies'.

working described here. But what does it really mean to use terms such as the 'art of child study' or also 'practical biography work'? This work was always carried out in groups. We sought to realize Steiner's concept of a 'research community'. In other words, everything we attempted to do was undertaken within the same group.

As far as 'practical biography work' is concerned, this meant that a member of the group of people working together over several years presented his own biography to the others as subject for research, 'made it available' one can say. First he would relate the story of his life, which the group then studied in terms of anthroposophic insights into human nature. In doing this we attempted two things: firstly, to get to know the person in question; and secondly, to verify and confirm the relevance of anthroposophic insights into the human being, which helped us to gain greater understanding and clarity about each person's biography. Our chief concern in this work was to base it *intrinsically* on a community endeavour. This was something we regarded as innovative.

It is self-apparent that this kind of procedure requires certain social skills of the participants. Any member of the group who did not possess these soon learned them, since self-correcting measures within a group are far more pronounced than in a lone individual.

It seems certain that this was one of the reasons why Rudolf Steiner envisaged such exercises for the work of the Society rather than of the School of Spiritual Science. It is a question here of learning in communities, working and researching collaboratively.

Applied to the 'art of child study', the relevance of community immediately appears obvious; for what is a college of teachers, a teachers' meeting, other than a research community? I am very well aware that many colleges and teachers' meetings are currently in a state of identity crisis. But the mode of working described here has frequently been shown to take effect very rapidly: it appears that *knowledge and insight* are precisely what enable *healing powers to flow out into the group or community*.

In publishing this book my hope is that many colleagues may experience this effect for themselves. It is one of anthroposophy's great secrets that knowledge and insight make us healthy, heal us in fact. If we regard the faculty or college of teachers as the heart of a school, the art of child study offers us an effective means to invigorate this heart.

But what does this mean for each individual and how does the art of child study live in the collegiate group? What quality does one need to observe and study children? In brief, the child study is actually nothing other than an *encounter* between people. But what constitutes it? How does it take place? Aside from the most superficial of all contacts between teachers and pupils, consisting of a kind of almost automatic, informational exchange such as 'Sit down!', 'Listen!', 'Please be quiet!', every encounter is a mystery of the I and thou. Martin Buber once wrote: 'The human being becomes an I through the thou.'

What am I meeting in such an encounter? A person's outward appearance? Certainly it starts with that. This can convey a great deal to me, though I can ignore or overlook its message and use appearance only to identify particular characteristics. Many encounters are like this. One registers an opposite number, and is then preoccupied only with what one's *own* psyche wishes to impart to the other.

It can however also happen that I myself awaken when I perceive the other person's appearance. What am I really seeing here, and what does this sight of another tell me? Do I have a tired, anxious, upset, happy, tense or expectant child in front of me? Do I meet a trusting or critical pupil here? What does his posture tell me? The colour of his skin? Do I have a healthy being before me, or one who seems ailing? What impression does this person make on me?

Insofar as we are aware of this, every perception and appearance elicits a feeling response in us, acts on a part of our soul life. Do I react to the person in front of me with restrained displeasure, or with my full sympathy? Or am I quite open to whatever I may find out, tinged, though, with a certain benevolence towards him? Or is this meeting with a pupil too much for me at present – am I over-stretched? Or is tangible anger even part of the picture perhaps?

Encounters can invoke every conceivable shade and nuance of feeling. But in all cases, when I meet another person, a process of self-perception begins. How am I behaving? What unexpressed yet real feelings are living in me? How clear am I in what I'm saying? Can I be myself, or is something mingling with me that is not really me, or that I do not wish to be?

The phenomenon of encounter in the child study is very different, and yet it possesses similar traits. The other, the subject of study, is not physically present, so the participants are looking at 'encounter residues'. Fragments of past encounters are related by colleagues. Previously accomplished acts are scrutinized: main lesson and school work, drawings, craft work, paintings, perhaps an essay: all these things bear witness to a person who is not even present in the room in an outward sense.

But at the same time the child study constructs in the souls of those present the presence, as image, of the living being of the child or adolescent. This is a significant, imaginative process, where everything remains invisible and yet is utterly real. If we participate authentically in this process, we can experience moments in it of existential importance for teachers, therapists, physicians and parents, for the whole school community and for the pupil himself. A *different kind of encounter* occurs.

After a session like this a person can feel that he was *touched* in a way that does not so easily happen in ordinary kinds of encounter.

One of the secondary effects of this 'different kind of encounter' can be the development of a new *sense of responsibility*. This suddenly awakens in relation to myself and to my actions as a human being and teacher. The fruit of this more intense preoccupation, the true encounter this makes possible, is that not only the other is changed, but above all I am myself.

Seen in this light, child studies are an indispensible tool for the whole school's development. We can even say that without the child study and the school development it cultivates, there will be no quality development; for ultimately quality is nothing other than *the sum of individual attitudes adopted by those involved in the educational process.*

This is a comforting thought, for everyone can, at any moment, embark on creating this reality.

This volume is dedicated to those who wish to do so.

II. INTRODUCTION

The archetype of the early days: Rudolf Steiner as leader and inspirer of the Stuttgart Waldorf School 1919–1924

It is Tuesday, 15 July, 1924. At around 8.30 in the evening, Rudolf Steiner calls an unscheduled teachers' meeting after receiving the bad news that two Class 11 pupils have been caught stealing. The theft is so serious that the youngsters will have to appear before the youth court.

Rudolf Steiner starts by checking his information about the incidents with that of the teachers. Then he launches into an analysis of the affair:

The pupils' intellectual development had been cultivated at the Waldorf School; they had made greater progress than at State school. From Class 8 or 9 onwards, as he put it, Waldorf pupils are a 'different type of young people' than is otherwise the case. But since we are whole human beings, this ongoing development should also include 'moral and soul' qualities. This, said Steiner, has not happened. Then he went on to explain that this state of affairs has 'been caused by circumstances', and can scarcely be radically improved 'if we have such overstretched teachers as currently'. And he continued: 'The kind of personal relationship with the children that would sustain moral and soul development alongside intellectual, mental development, has been lacking. From Class 8 onwards, there is a very apparent lack of teachers' moral influence on the pupils.' The pupils, he said, were 'left to their own devices as far as moral guidance is concerned', and 'the way teachers spoke about pupils showed that they had not established this moral connection with them'.[1]

Furthermore, he said, someone had written him a letter about this matter in which he did not discern the existence of any human relationship between the teachers and the pupils involved. And thus he had concluded that in faculty meetings he himself had been unable to attend, teachers had not concerned themselves with elaborating 'psychological pictures' to develop their understanding of the pupils' personalities. No 'pupil psychology' had been developed; and in summary he stated: 'Pupils in higher classes with especially marked individual characteristics ought to have been the subject of teachers' studies.'

In the next stage of this difficult meeting, Steiner made up for the lost ground in exemplary fashion, presenting three detailed accounts of the pupils involved in the theft, and describing what one could have done and should do to help these adolescents progress in their development in a way that had not so far happened.

This meeting was the second to last of those Steiner attended; in dramatic circumstances, therefore, it contains three 'psychological pictures' which can in a sense can be seen as a kind of legacy to us for the practice of child studies.

Early child studies

Looking back to the school's founding phase five years earlier, a meeting was held on 8 September 1919 to deal with more formal matters of timetables and substitute teachers. The school premises were not quite ready yet. Steiner had to leave on a trip and was therefore not present when the school started on 16 September. But on the 25th he returned to Stuttgart, took a look at the classes and the lessons being given, and sat down with the teachers to hold two important meetings (on 25 and 26 September). In these first meetings, based only on ten days' experience (!) of teaching in the school, Steiner was asked many questions about individual pupils. In those early days the questions often had a very elementary character, such as: 'I have a child in Class 6 who really struggles, but does not disturb the lessons. (...) I would like to try to keep him in the class.' Or: 'I have a boy in Class 8 who is melancholic, and pretty backward. I'd like to send him back to Class 7.' Such statements show us something of the nature of those times, the inexperience of these first teachers, and no doubt also their sense of helplessness ('My Class 5 yell and make a racket, especially in language lessons. They find the French phrases comical.')

In retrospect we can only admire their courage. After only two weeks of preparation, the twelve of them had to give lessons to 256 pupils and get the whole school running smoothly.

In this exemplary, innovative situation, we can recognize a fundamental gesture of key importance: the teachers take their concerns and difficulties to the teachers' meeting. It was quite natural for them to do so, justified as they were in hoping for ready, copious help from the school's director Rudolf Steiner. In this very first period, therefore, the child study developed in archetypal form. Concerns and questions were taken to the community; and expectations of finding a response to them there were met since Steiner was able to offer answers.

But what happens when Steiner cannot answer because he is absent? As we know, he had many other tasks. What conditions need to be created so that one's questions, difficulties and concerns can be entrusted to the community of colleagues?

This question leads us to the first lecture of *The Foundations of Human Experience*.[2] Rudolf Steiner begins with the following, somewhat surprising words:

> My dear friends, we will only be equal to our task if we do not regard it only as a comfortable intellectual undertaking, but instead as being moral and spiritual in the most eminent sense ...

Here again, therefore, he accentuates the moral and spiritual dimension. We can see that these are not empty words from the second* inaugural meeting of 26 September 1919. Shortly before he ends the meeting, and reminds the teachers of the possibility of ongoing spiritual collaboration with him despite his absence, he sums up his experience of visiting classes after the first ten days of the school's existence, when it had eight classes:

> The most important thing is to ensure contact is always kept alive: that the teacher forms a real unity with the pupils. Basically I found that this does exist in nearly every class, in a very fine, pleasing way. I was very pleased to see this.[3]

But can we define the nature of this 'moral' dimension in pedagogical terms? A key aspect here is that teachers do not approach their pupils with a distancing stance but that they encompass the children and adolescents in a way that gives rise to a 'unity' – so that pupils and teachers live and work *together* and not just alongside or even in opposition to each other.

Repeatedly one can feel surprised, even greatly struck to discover the way all Steiner's comments and suggestions are closely interwoven, and the lack of any discrepancy between them. For instance, if one compares the opening sentence quoted above from *The Foundations of Human Experience* with the teacher's seven virtues which he impresses on future teachers

---

* Discounting the first meeting on practical and administrative matters.

at the very end of the same book, we discover a helpful correspondence. The third of these virtues, states Steiner is: 'Sharpen your inner feeling of responsibility.'* What does this signify? It ask us to recognize that as teachers we bear responsibility not only for imparting knowledge but, above and beyond this, along with others, for our pupil's inner, soul development. In other words, we cannot be indifferent to our pupils as human beings. And in fact we have shared responsibility for accompanying them, guiding them into life and into a sense of who they are; and for helping them value this process. Naturally – even if this is not so apparent at first – pupils and their teacher have a shared destiny for a considerable portion of their lives. Destiny arises here, even if a teacher fails to acknowledge this.

In trying to picture this moral context, we can find that it kindles our motivation as teachers rather than weighing on us. Spirit knowledge, as real practice, works in this way. It is not theoretical.

Yet as the Waldorf school developed and the years passed, it became evident that this expectation could not be met. What Steiner regarded, and repeatedly emphasized, as being of key importance, was not realized to a sufficient degree. Instead there were three distinct systems: teachers, teaching content and pupils. Although Steiner kept trying to highlight this problem of 'separate systems' from various angles, things did

---

* Translated in *The Foundations* … as: 'Sharpen your feeling for responsibility of soul.'

not change initially. But looking back at this early history, what was achieved still seems astonishing. The first teachers' only preparation had been to attend Rudolf Steiner's two-week course. Otherwise they were equipped only with their own enthusiasm and will. While these first colleagues were all very educated people, and strongly anchored in anthroposophy, this new form of education in which they had to draw entirely on their own resources was something they were not yet able to master in all its details, even if they did have intuitive knowledge of how to go about it. For many of them, this new art of education involved battling with their own previous schooling and upbringing, and the constitutions they had acquired in consequence.

These factors, their own conditioning, had to be transformed into entirely new forms of pedagogical conduct, and it is self-evident this could only happen through profound crises. But these teachers were willing to go through this; and Steiner himself was aware of what it would mean. Even before the school opened, he spoke of the initiative as his 'problem child'.

It is truly miraculous that the movement for a new type of education emerged from this seed, and has come to be effective and highly regarded in all parts of the globe. The question still remains, however, to what extent the three basic aspects of the educational process have succeeded in forming a harmonious, unified mutual relationship.

The prompting to develop a psychology, and 'psychological pictures'

In the summer and autumn of 1920, Steiner identifies a further problem he sees as connected with the school's identity. In June 1920, and at the meeting on 23 September, he first praises the school's progress, then adds however:

> It is always the case that progressive aspects will increasingly correspond in coming years to the ideas connected with the Waldorf school. [...] What I mean is this: In future we must place increasing importance on psychology. Work psychologically! I don't mean this in as abstract or theoretical way as it might seem. It sounds as if one wishes to psychoanalyze the children. But when you accustom yourself to making real efforts to get to know the children psychologically, you gradually form a different relationship with them, simply as outcome of such endeavour. Getting to know them more deeply does not just mean recognizing their characteristics; a different relationship arises with them when you try to get to know them better. [...] To gain psychological insight into children's real nature is something that can only be achieved through hard study.
>
> After our first years of work, I believe this is one of the things we should now regard as central: learning to understand the children, and never thinking they ought to be a certain, predetermined way.[4]

At this point Steiner is aware of the risk he is running when he uses the term 'psychology'. He tries, as we see, to distance himself from a common understanding of the term as 'analysis'. Instead of this, by using the word which refers to the soul or psyche, and speaking of 'getting to know' children, he is actually embarking in a quite different direction: one immediately founded on a tangible relationship between two individuals.

In fact we touch here on a key problem with a significant epistemological background. If we consider our capacity of perception for a moment, we can ask what enables us to grasp a flowering horse chestnut tree in spring *as* a horse chestnut tree. It is easy to recognize that a long process involving perception, memory, and conceptualization has to precede this certainty, and then allows us to state almost instinctively what it is we see. It would take the scope of a whole book to determine whether perceiving the chestnut tree is a matter of practice, a recalled connection between perception and concept, or whether we could say even that this perception is the physical confirmation of a conceptual idea of the horse chestnut.

The following question is significant here: Is a lion at the zoo *the* lion, or only the visible illustration of its species? I cannot see a species as such, but only think it. This problem contains something important that will also play a role in child studies. Horse chestnut and lion are easy to define for, from a certain standpoint, they are straightforward and easily comprehensible.

But what do I see if I picture a child, a pupil to myself (not analytically but in the sense Steiner urges of 'getting to know' him)? What do we see? If we are rigorously honest about it, we have to say: not much!

In purely outward terms we ascertain whether the pupil is tall or short, fat or thin, blond or dark-haired; how he stands and walks. And that's about it. Thankfully, since we don't suffer from agnosia, his features quickly tell us he is Fred. Yet recognizing Fred in this way is doing no more than recognizing a lion at the zoo: as an example of his 'species'. But what species does Fred belong to? To none! Fred is unmistakably Fred, and there isn't another one of him. Nevertheless, without much difficulty, but without grasping the species Fred, I recognize him as an example of humanity.

It is this path Steiner pursues in speaking of 'getting to know' children, when he says,

> Getting to know them more deeply does not just mean recognizing their characteristics; a different relationship arises with them when you try to get to know them better. [...] To gain psychological insight into children's real nature is something that can only be achieved through hard study.

As if in a landscape briefly illumined by lightning, the whole art of child study is encapsulated in these words. To become acquainted with a child, in this sense, is to seek ways to understand the unique being concealed within every pupil. Such developing acquaintance has the quality of insight, of deeper perception, rather than a merely superficial recording of information. Precisely because deeper insight is involved here, we can use it to help our children and pupils in whatever way they need. The early development of the Waldorf school in Stuttgart, however, shows how difficult Steiner found it to elicit any understanding for this amongst the teachers.

Exactly a year later, in connection with problems that surfaced in Class 10, Steiner again highlights the distance between teachers and pupils when he says that teachers are 'lecturing' rather than teaching.[5]

The crisis that erupts in the autumn of 1923 turns on two decisive pivots: the teachers' moral stance to and relationship with the pupils – or in other words the lack of real contact between them – and a lecture-style of teaching that is too academic (nowadays we would say 'one-way communication').

The 'unity' of teachers and pupils, and connection with the subject as the life blood of Waldorf education

In the following summer of 1924, problems relating to the 'disunity' between teachers and pupils surfaced once again. Below, Steiner poses this existential question, albeit in veiled form. Referring to the pupils' moral frame of mind and soul, he says (author's emphases):

We have to look these things squarely in the face in their whole psychological intensity. We will have to give serious consideration to overcoming these problems **if the Waldorf School is to survive.** The good will of all must work together, starting perhaps – **if the Waldorf School is to continue** – with a series of teachers' meetings **before the school's new beginning** to agree the school's moral stance and outlook, as indispensible undertaking. We will not make any headway otherwise. There is a great deficiency here.[6]

This paragraph suggests that in Rudolf Steiner's view the change needed is so radical that the school must contemplate a whole new beginning if it is to continue to exist. And this new beginning would be marked by more intensive contact with pupils on the part of teachers: a new cultivation of the moral connection with them. This, he says, is necessary 'if the Waldorf school is to survive'.

As the meeting progresses, Steiner speaks of how pained he is by these matters. ('This is really weighing on me; so you see, this has grieved me sorely.') He continually reiterates his experience that the 'academic tone' of the teaching has become more pronounced, if anything, rather than diminishing, and urges the faculty to 'Speak out and say whatever you wish'.

Yet as if the whole tragedy of the situation has simply passed these teachers by, one of them then asks: 'What kind of constitution do these children have?' This comment is incontrovertible evidence of the deficiencies Steiner had been highlighting so fulsomely for years now: the pupil is regarded from a distance, rather than with inner participation. There is a lack of empathy, of connection with the human other.

Subsequently Steiner brings things to a head: '**I have**

to give a new impetus here.' The teachers, he says, lack interest in the pupils, and lack enthusiasm for their own teaching. Lessons are given in a 'weary' way: 'A person must not be weary if he is to live in the spirit.' And he goes on:

> To gain psychological pictures of the pupils requires sophisticated pedagogical skills, and this is what I'd like to discuss. But of prime importance are enthusiasm and interest.

Steiner now resolves to undertake a new set of tasks for the forthcoming autumn: a new impetus in which the art and skills of child study are to be further developed, governed entirely by interest in the pupils, and enthusiasm for the teacher's work.

Rudolf Steiner's last comment, in the last general faculty meeting of 3 September 1924, is especially moving in this regard:

> In September or the first week in October I want to give lectures on **the moral aspects of education and teaching**.

But Rudolf Steiner's illness and unexpected, premature death meant that he could no longer do this.

These occurrences, if we ponder them, can tell us that in the dramatic, tragic situation right at the end of Steiner's life, child studies (or the lack of them) played a key role in the first Waldorf School.

At times when Steiner could not take part in faculty meetings due to other obligations, the teachers had failed to bring to the meetings their concerns, questions and problems with pupils; and thus no corresponding 'psychological pictures' of the children were formed.

Steiner connects the lack of such dialogue in his absence with a lack of interest in the teachers for individual pupils. Here he uses the word 'interest' in the sense of understanding and empathy for another. Through interest one can come to understand pupils; and specifically through this intensified activity, this focused, open attentiveness, what one can call the school's unity develops: a wholeness of community between teachers and children. The child study is an important tool for creating this unified context. Steiner refers to this whole complex, along with the teachers' lively interest in and commitment to their own teaching, as the 'spiritual, moral context' – and by this he does not mean spiritual or meditative activity but the shared life and work of teachers and pupils.

The crisis of those days happened ninety years ago. Nevertheless, we can see that in many schools the child study has lapsed almost entirely and been forgotten. Today only very few faculties still attend to the pupils in this way as part of their accustomed 'quality routines', connecting with the children by this means and of course developing and enhancing their own skills at the same time, to create this much-needed unity between teachers and pupils.

The present volume aims to help rediscover this wonderful tool of the child study so that it can come into full use again. Today, when so many pupils bring complex constitutions with them, it offers a genuine form of quality assurance: not one based on external measures or checklists, but arising instead from a capacity and skill that teachers develop together. In this way the teachers' meeting can become a research community once again.

Defining terms

The introduction has given a historical survey of the child study, showing how intrinsic this mode of faculty work is to the Waldorf school, and what happened already in the founding period when this work was neglected. I have used certain key terms: *interest* in pupils, *enthusiasm for teaching*, and the phrase *psychological pictures* – or in other words the development of a child or pupil psychology. Below I would now like to define these terms a little more precisely.

Interest in pupils

It would be a very strange teacher who said that he wasn't interested in his pupils. But this superficial daily interest in pupils is not what is meant here; rather it refers to an interest that leads to understanding: a deeper interest that gives insight, enabling the teacher to properly perceive the child, and thus also address him fully. Here's a simple example: a teacher who has perceived and pondered on a pupil's temperament through this deeper kind of interest – which is always also a form of research and enquiry – will speak to him in a different way from someone to whom the child's temperament remains hidden. The pupil will experience the teacher as a less alien and intrusive presence if the latter can quite naturally consider and draw upon the child's temperament. Interest is the prerequisite for understanding the other, in turn developing our capacity for relationship.

Enthusiasm

We would be misreading Steiner if we thought his reference to enthusiasm indicated some brief flare or flash-in-the-pan. Rather, he sees it as the existential lifeblood of all teaching. Enthusiasm is a power kindled when the teacher has made the teaching material his own to such a degree that he himself is 'tinged' by the subject matter. The teacher is a different person when he teaches maths from when he teaches history, and different again in turn when he teaches a foreign language. This self-transformation through the subject is thus an expression of enthusiasm for teaching. This quality comes to the fore in the upper school especially in what we may call 'authenticity' – that is, the accord between our personality, our mastery of the subject and our mode of presentation. Great emphasis should be placed on this quality. At pre-school age, it involves the teacher's capacity to fully affirm the children's being.

Psychology and psychological pictures

As we can tell from Steiner's words on this subject, the term 'psychology' is not used here in the orthodox way, nor does it refer to educational psychology in the commonly accepted sense. Instead, Steiner is here concerned in a far more fundamental and practical way with a capacity the teacher develops through intensive study of anthroposophically oriented insights into human nature. While this does not necessarily exclude concepts enshrined in orthodox psychology, it is, more importantly, a stance in which we do not *distance ourselves* from the other, but relate to him *feelingly and empathically*. Ever and again Steiner urges his teachers to 'become psychologists', to 'write the golden book of psychology'. If we study these suggestions in detail, it becomes clear that the term psychology is used here in a very lively way, and could also be defined as 'acting out of understanding'. But this also means that the teacher adopts an inclusive stance: together with the pupils he forms part of the process of education; and thus pupils and teachers are not in a divided, subject-object relationship but always participate in a single 'we'.

Now it is true – we might say in a Goethean sense – that we can only study and understand the developing child if we can be keenly interested in him.[7] While such interest must seek objectivity, it also needs to be always warmly enveloped in understanding and sympathy – not personal, instinctive sympathy but one which the teacher has acquired as conscious capacity: a fundamental sympathy for everything human. Steiner's concept of psychology is therefore not abstract or analytic but all-embracing, holistic, incredibly down-to-earth and practical.

The details of this approach will later be elaborated further; but meanwhile we can regard what has been stated here as the key foundation, the mood and character, of the art of child study. Without the enveloping warmth of universal human love, such work could easily lead to (potentially dismissive) value judgements about a pupil, and thus not only be wounding but entirely fail to achieve its aim.

Yet a child study can trigger a significant and enthusiastic impetus if teachers succeed in speaking together, in a focused way, about the child concerned. The experience that something *important* has been done together awakens confidence and trust in the community. Child studies are practical applications of anthroposophy's 'new psychology'. And the experience that anthroposophic insights are not merely theoretical but of real practical use and worth is one of the sources of empowerment and rejuvenation acknowledged by everyone who has ever participated in a child study with real commitment.

III. BASES FOR THE ART OF CHILD STUDY

The meetings of 1924 as background to the origins of the child study

From the Christmas Foundation Meeting of 1923/24, when Rudolf Steiner re-founded the General Anthroposophical Society in Dornach, Switzerland, anthroposophy's form (the Society itself) and its content ('teachings') were henceforth one. This was a new founding insofar as Steiner had until then worked in the Anthroposophical Society only as a teacher and adviser; but now he took the affairs of the Society into his own hand: he became its chairman in the hope that the vessel (the Society itself) might bring anthroposophy to expression in all its undertakings. Steiner coined a particular term for this process: from now on everything was to have an 'esoteric character'. In other words, every action was to be the expression of living spirit, and this was true for both the most spiritual and most earthly deeds enacted by this Society in future. At this conference, therefore, an appeal went out to members to consider anthroposophy as a path of schooling, one that must also be practised when representing anthroposophy in the public domain. Steiner wanted everything emerging from anthroposophy to see the light of day and not remain hidden. For many of those who attended, this conference marked the birth of a new culture; and the understanding of spiritual science that emerged from it has remained the source of spiritual science's endeavour and striving to this day.[8]

Some of the teachers at the Stuttgart Waldorf School also returned from the Christmas Foundation Meeting with a strong new impulse. When Steiner got back to Stuttgart to discuss the school's progress at faculty meetings, they asked him whether, given the new situation, it might be a good idea for him to become the school's official director.

Steiner rejected this idea. He was, he said, an adviser to the school, and every individual was free to accept his advice. He regarded himself as a member of the college of teachers, of the faculty. Nowadays we might say that he was the 'first among equals' ('Primus inter pares' in the Latin phrase). Steiner also dismissed the idea of the teachers collectively affiliating with the Society's newly founded School of Spiritual Science, saying that freedom was integral to the Waldorf school, and that it was therefore not an organ of the School of Spiritual Science. He repeatedly emphasized that while the Waldorf school lived by virtue of anthroposophy, it was not an organ of the General Anthroposophical Society.

Thus work recommenced. The teachers became members of the School of Spiritual Science only by the individual resolve of each.[9]

We need to include all this if we wish to understand

the teachers' meetings held in Steiner's day. From the very outset the principle of collegiality, and collegial responsibility was paramount for him:

> The schools will be set up and administered not hierarchically but in a republican fashion. In a true republic of teachers we'll have nothing to recline on comfortably in the form of decrees issued by a directorate; but instead we will have to give to our work what enables each one of us to take full responsibility for our undertakings. Each and every person must take responsibility himself.[10]

From such responsibility two possibilities emerge. Depending on one's individual capacities of self-reflection or self-knowledge, a view can form that one is equal – or not – to such responsibility. Usually we feel equal to taking responsibility if we know (roughly) what we need to do, and how we can respond to situations; and when we find that we can gradually realize the goals we have set ourselves. In this case we feel we're 'in the flow', and that life is, if you like, meeting us halfway.

But if we don't feel equal to the responsibility, we are unsure what should be done in any situation, and the pupil or pupils remain a riddle to us. The goals we are aiming for are not achieved, and we feel 'stuck'. The process, the next step, the sense of progressing, comes to a standstill. Uncertainty arises, and a sense of discrepancy between life and our tasks.

If we give serious thought to Steiner's statements about a form of governance that operates through each individual's sense of responsibility, as opposed to one dispensed hierarchically, in specific terms this can only mean that we take our difficulties and problems with pupils or with the teaching content (i.e. our own inability to meet our responsibilities) to the teachers' meeting, and ask our colleagues (the republic of teachers) for advice. No doubt this is an idea that takes some getting used to. But this is likely to have been still harder in the past. There were generations of teachers who could not abide the idea of having done something imperfectly or, worse still, being unable to do something. If a problem surfaced that could not be ignored, this was naturally not of one's own making but was caused by others – the pupils for instance. (You always see this stance at work when teachers complain or moan vociferously about children. If you ask them whether they'd consider having a child study on the pupil(s) in question, you find they decline the suggestion.)

In the meantime, our general level of self-awareness has progressed: someone who cultivates self-knowledge on a regular basis knows that he does things wrong. Naturally there's a limit to our skills; but we can try to improve. And this is far more important, because it gives rise to a new social gesture: that of giving and receiving help without losing our self-esteem. When this kind of inner stance holds sway, the teachers' meeting suddenly becomes fluid and dynamic, for now the individual with his own concerns is not the sole focus but instead colleagues are working together as a community on the common educational task.

Examples from the faculty meetings with Rudolf Steiner

Today, reading the three volumes of faculty meetings with Rudolf Steiner, we can see that the teachers asked him numerous questions: frequently about the curriculum ('What ought I to read in English lessons in Class 8?') or general pedagogical questions. Steiner replies in great practical detail. For example:

> For this maths teaching I would ask you to take the main lesson periods for adding new themes, where you continue and develop the subject; but use two separate half-hour lessons each week to repeat what has been learned in main lesson.[11]

Or:

> In the higher classes the principle of 'lecturing' at students has crept in, and lessons have become more a matter of sensation. They [do not?] listen, they don't work inwardly on what they hear, and are therefore not developing adequate skills.[12]

Alongside this, advice was given about working with individual pupils with whom the teachers were having difficulties. For instance, if a teacher asked for advice in the meeting because he didn't know how to help a child, Rudolf Steiner would observe a lesson with the child and come back to the next meeting with advice. This advice would be kept brief, and a child study of this kind usually lasted only a few minutes. To examine this more closely, I will cite an example from the meeting on 26 May 1920 (CW 300 a):

> Several children in Class 5 are discussed, especially E. E.
>
> **Teacher:** He's not keeping up with the rest. He's gifted in languages. He's crafty and cunning.
>
> **Steiner:** Taking his personality into account as much as possible, it would be good to occupy him now and then, stimulate him. Then you should vary it, should repeatedly give him special attention.
>
> **Teacher:** Shouldn't he go to the support class?
>
> **Steiner:** What would he do there? He's a real eccentric. It would make more of an impression on him if you get him to make a pair of shoes. One should get him to bang nails in, and learn to make shoes. Make a proper pair of boots for someone else. Get E. to make shoes in handwork: that would help. He'd enjoy that: soling shoes, making double soles.

From the meeting on 28 October 1922 (CW 300 b):

> **Teacher:** P. Z. in 4b disrupts the class, makes unnecessary remarks.
>
> **Steiner:** Besides treating him with eurythmy therapy, you could perhaps also get him to retell stories

that reflect his own behaviour, in whose narrative he himself comes to seem absurd. Try to weave into a story a remark such as those he makes; in which someone gets a soaking because of the remark he makes, or some such incident …

A teacher talks about L. K. in Class 1. She cannot bear to hear fairytales, or poems either.

Steiner: She should do I (ee) with her whole body, U (oo) with her ears and index finger, E (eh) with her hair, so that in all three exercises sensitivity enters her in some degree. Awaken her body's sensitivity. This would need to be done over a longer period.[13]

These examples are illustrative of many others. The pattern is always the same: teachers ask questions and Steiner replies. In the next section we will take a closer look at the nature of his replies. First, though, let us just observe that the pattern is simple and straightforward: someone asks a question and receives an answer. We see not just an adviser at work but someone with outstanding capacities and knowledge. We can encapsulate this in an image: the teachers in a circle and Steiner in the middle; the teachers asking questions and receiving answers. The questions come from the collegiate 'periphery' while the answers come from the 'centre'.

Then a new situation arises: Rudolf Steiner falls ill, and from the autumn of 1925 is no longer available to help. The teachers are now thrown back on their own resources and promptings.[14] How does this alter the picture? The group of teachers gather to discuss a child. What is at the centre now? The question itself; and the

Teachers   **Teachers**

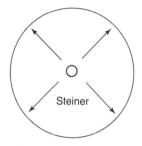
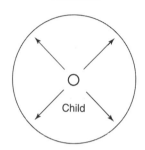

Steiner teaches the teachers
to understand the child

The child teaches the teachers
to understand him

'periphery' must answer. In the case of a child study, the child himself is at the centre, and the periphery ponders the answer. An inversion has taken place.

Why is it important to attend to this inversion process? In my view something significant arises here. We experience the teachers' meeting as the soul of the school, its heart. A heart, too, can learn, and wishes to. We can regard the child study not only as necessary for helping a child and his teacher, but as simultaneously providing a wonderful learning impulse for the *whole* faculty. Seen and practised in this way, the faculty meeting can become a 'high school of psychology' (Steiner) in which the group of teachers continually educates itself. If we see the described inversion in very real and tangible terms, it can certainly give us pause for reflection: wisdom and help originally flowed from a centre to the periphery, where the help given was taken up as far as possible. Now the question itself has become the centre, and the periphery must develop the capacity to give wisdom and help.

For this to happen, a broader concept of the teachers' meeting is needed.

Broadening our view of the teachers' meeting

It has become customary to regard the teachers' meeting as a forum for the exchange of factual information; and this 'business meeting' often takes precedence over pedagogical issues. Naturally this function of the meeting is important and necessary, but it loses its justification if it suppresses the *pedagogical* meeting. The pedagogical meeting is the heart of the school, where discussions are held on a 'republican' footing – that is, between equals – on questions of pedagogy and daily life in the educational realm.

It seems to me that we need a renewal of the idea of this meeting and its place in the school, so that colleagues are not obliged to undertake their pedagogical work in small groups outside the school, as if in exile.

How can the pedagogical meeting work effectively? The conditions needed for preparing child studies

A new view of the importance of the teachers' meeting will draw on commitment to the pedagogical meeting within the school. Speaking of the teachers' meeting on various occasions,[15] Steiner uses the terms 'soul' and 'heart' in regard to the faculty or college meeting on pedagogical matters, which, by his suggestion, should if possible take place on Thursdays.[16] If the school's administrative governance is separate from the pedagogical meeting, it can be good for the school's manager to take over these tasks. But the school organism still needs a heart, a core organ, with functions at a psychological and human level comparable to the heart's physiological functions. A comparison with the picture of the heart reveals four qualities:

1. Mutual awareness
Mutual awareness means more than just sharing information. In this context a college of teachers will not merely *meet* once a week, but will seek to *encounter and engage with* each other. This means experiencing one another, attending to what lives in the others. Looking back together over the events of the past week, they listen to each another and engage in dialogue. A wide range of different experiences and intentions here resonate together and come to shared expression.

2. Finding common views
The faculty has to work its way through to insights and decisions. For example: Ought there to be two classes for a particular year; or should we organize language teaching differently? How do we feel about the timetable – is it sufficiently expansive or does it seem a little breathless? How do we wish the outside world to see us, and how do we need to be seen? In other words, the

community of teachers discusses things together, forming common views in all kinds of areas. This is already important enough. Yet the inner aspect of this process is of still greater significance: the practice of formulating shared views as a whole *community*. What is needed to achieve this? An alert sense of one's own responsibility and, equally, of the limits of this responsibility. It is very important, for example, for an individual to be clear about the issues where he has nothing to contribute and should only listen. Each person must sense where he needs to be involved and where he should hold back.

3. Learning together

If teaching presupposes self-education,[17] then the teacher *must* engage his or her will to learn from *every situation*. And the concentrated sum of such will involves ongoing further education within the college. It was Steiner's wish that *teachers' faculty meetings* should represent a 'pinnacle' of applied psychology.

This field also encompasses child and class studies: not as decision-making processes but as a *learning process*. To deepen insight into the nature of the human being (i.e. anthropology) and to help and support pupils (and thus one's colleagues also) contributes substantially to quality assurance in a school. Where a school works in accordance with such principles, the Waldorf school becomes what it was originally conceived to be: a school for *all* children.

4. Finding common initiative

Decisions made together in faculty meetings are of

great importance for the whole life of the school. In regard to mundane matters, this is just daily business. But here I wish to point to a more general level of initiative. Which direction are we heading in as a whole school and what do we wish to achieve together? What are our pedagogical and spiritual goals? In what inner direction does the whole school wish to develop? Does the faculty meeting devote time to such considerations, or do endless mundane matters overburden its agenda? It sometimes almost seems as if the culture of dealing with daily practical business is a way to *avoid* engaging with the school's real concerns. Almost instinctively we evade the really important things.

The first condition for a child study is therefore to establish a *pedagogical meeting* in the school, which in some form or other undertakes its task of creating a centre and community, rather than obstructing this.

Practice has shown that a second group of conditions exist, and make the whole child study process easier. Lying in the social domain, they are well worth cultivating. While the child study itself should not become an over-formalized procedure, observing the following is extremely helpful.

Preparing the child study

1. The need for someone to chair the discussion
The child study needs a chairperson. This doesn't have to be the chair of college, nor does the class teacher

of the child in question have to take on this role. The important thing is that the chairperson has the ability to create the right equilibrium between a rigorously conducted discussion with clear *guidelines* and a *free and open exchange*. He has to be able to establish this fine balance. This also requires the chairperson to have a knack for sensing where the discussion is heading while always keeping the child's being clearly in view.

2. *The involvement of all colleagues*
Rudolf Steiner always stressed that teachers should avoid becoming too specialized.[18] In relation to the child study this means that teachers who do *not* know the child should also be involved in the discussion. Those who do not teach the child often turn out to have helpful questions and valuable advice to offer. And colleagues who attend to the discussion with great interest but without any spoken contribution, can help create the right underlying mood. As a matter of principle it makes sense for **all colleagues to attend the child study.** This is apparent too from the archetype of the child study, its original form as initiated by Steiner in the college of teachers of the first Waldorf school. This does not mean however that discussions about a child cannot also be held in smaller groups of teachers for specific purposes.

3. *The virtue of reticence*
The following is also an important condition for a successful child study. In every faculty are colleagues who have engaged more profoundly than others with

anthroposophic insights into the human being; and in every child study, likewise, there will be teachers who know more about the child in question than others. It is these two categories of teachers, above all, who should practise reticence during the study. This may sound paradoxical; yet if we take the picture of the circle seriously, we can see that either of the two types of colleagues described could, in their enthusiasm, easily influence the course of discussion in a one-sided way. The important thing, in fact, is to allow a basis of discussion to emerge from the whole group of teachers.[19]

4. How long should a child study last?

There are faculties that take two meetings for a child study; some even customarily take three. While this is a very fine endeavour, the success of this work is entirely dependent on the degree to which colleagues succeed in really devoting their thoughts to the child over a week (or two), or in other words, maintaining their attentiveness. A child study in several parts only succeeds if this is so. Usually, though, circumstances mean that it is very difficult to keep a child alive in one's thoughts through a whole week. If this attentiveness, as the basis for engagement with the child, is not maintained, at the second meeting after a week one can often find that the 'picture' of the child has faded and that really one has to start again from scratch. I therefore recommend doing a child study in one go, i.e. taking around an hour and a quarter for it. This also demands **presence of mind**. People often stay that it is good to 'sleep on things' for a night. While this is true (though you have to *do* something too, and not just sleep), experience has shown that the quality of the focus in the group of colleagues is of prime importance. Once a group of teachers has acquired a certain facility in the practice of child study, they will notice moments occurring when things intensify and become more tangible: a sense that there is more reality in the room than usual.

5. The role of parents
It is often asked whether the **parents** of a child should attend the child study. If the school has developed to the point where parents can do this, it is good. But this depends on the whole atmosphere. How does the school organism relate to parents? Is there a fundamental sense of openness between them? Or is there uneasiness, unexpressed tensions? Whether or not parents attend depends on such factors. At all events, the child study should be undertaken *as if* the parents were present.

Parents must always be **asked in advance** whether they agree to their child being discussed at the meeting. (The class teacher or school doctor will anyway usually need to speak with them beforehand.) It is morally tactful for parents to know that the teachers will be focusing their attention on the child for a period, so that they can stand behind this. The aim, after all, is to help and support the child. Since parent-teacher relationships can be so diverse, what has been stated here should always be interpreted according to the prevailing realities. Social tact is involved.

6. Our inner stance during a child study

In the child study discussion, whatever is said should be spoken with the greatest possible sense of responsibility towards the pupil, **as if he himself were present.** A teacher would do better to keep silent than to give his feelings free rein. Furthermore it is self-evident that the discussion does not continue over coffee. The child study should be kept within its 'sacred' bounds as a specially designated time.

7. Handling the outcomes of the child study

A faculty of teachers helps take itself seriously if it asks a colleague to record the **outcomes** of the child study in writing. Looking back a few weeks later, and recalling the outcomes (consisting, of course, of tasks for the teachers), we can then check whether what we undertook to do has been done; and whether this has had a positive effect on the child. This brief review is a learning moment for all involved. Have we done what we agreed, and did it work? If not, what went wrong and how? A review of this kind is a means of assuring quality in our work.

8. Presence of mind

Finally, a word about listening and speaking. Both require special cultivation in the child study. One commonly observes that some colleagues never say anything while others always do. In the child study it is very important to develop a sense of the **right moment** to make one's own contribution. Is it needed now or not? Is what one wishes to say going to serve the process, or is it just about getting something off one's chest? The same applies to listening. There is a very intent kind of listening, in which one is fully present and engaged; but also a silence that is really inner absence. In the latter case, a dead point exists within the collegial group and exerts its negative effect.

IV. STRUCTURE OF A CHILD STUDY

Having considered the preparatory conditions let us now turn to the actual form and process of a child study. I'd like to preface this by saying again that a child study should *not* become formalized or rigid in its procedures. This may sound astonishing, but every child creates the form he needs. Any rigid adherence to a predetermined programme or schedule would therefore be alien to the spirit of the undertaking and detrimental to it. Indeed, this would hinder and stultify our creative capacities for seeing each pupil anew.

Anyone practising the art of child study will find that it inevitably has three stages. These three steps can be described as follows:

1. *Forming a picture*
2. *Finding causes*
3. *Finding remedies*

Naturally one can also find other terms for this process.

1. Forming a picture

How can we form a picture of the child, and what is involved in doing so? As an example, at the meeting a week prior to the child study, the child's class teacher can announce that he intends discussing this child at the next meeting. His initiative here is founded on questions that he cannot resolve alone. This prior notification need take no more than five minutes. In advance of this, ideally, the school doctor (who may be present) will have examined the child from his medical perspective, and the teacher will also have discussed the matter with the child's parents. Colleagues who do not teach the class in question thus have an opportunity to observe him at play times during the following week. Here too, tact is called for. How do I observe a child, a fellow human being, and keep this a 'pure' undertaking, using my senses only to learn more and to help the child develop in positive ways? In other words, this is not about my own personal predilections or, still worse, my value judgements. A scrutinizing look founded on a cool, detached stance, with little empathy, can come close to personal insult if it does not fully serve the aim of helping the child by furthering one's understanding of him. Great moral tact is required here.

Based on colleagues' perception and awareness of the child during the week, the child study meeting begins the following week. To start with, the class teacher describes the child as succinctly as possible. Here it helps to divide this description into two aspects: the pupil's **spatial form** on the one hand, and his **temporal form** on the other.

The spatial form

What does the child look like? If he were standing in the room, what would be particularly noticeable about him? Is there anything unique or very distinctive in his form? Is he tall, athletic or delicate, slender, perhaps even thin? Or does he look strong, sturdy, perhaps on the small side and/or even stocky? Is the overall impression of his bodily form balanced and harmonious? How does his head 'sit' on the trunk: light and mobile; or as if stuck on, with a short neck? Are his limbs short or long in relation to his trunk?

Let's consider his head first of all. How does the threefold quality of forehead, nose and eyes, and chin express itself? Does the chin jut forward, or are his nose and eyes accentuated? What quality appears in his forehead?

At this phase of the study, we are primarily concerned with overall impressions: how does this human being stand in the world?

The temporal form

In looking at the temporal form of the child we consider his development. How has his life been up to now? What experiences has he had? How does he behave, and what are his skills and habits? Are his movements noticeable in some way? How does he walk? Is his step heavy or light? Does he stamp on the ground as he walks, or do his feet scarcely touch the earth? Do his heels come down energetically on the ground or does he seem to hover on his tip-toes? Are his movements 'angular' or fluid? What comes to expression in the child's life up to now?

There are children who live in the same house, in the same place until they leave home, while others have already moved home five times by the time they are ten. What family constellation surrounds the child? Is he the eldest child, second, middle or youngest in the family? (In fact it is a good idea to consider the whole class in these terms. Is there a wide cross-section of pupils as regards their family placing, or do a great many youngest, eldest or middle children predominate?)

The temporal form of the child should also include consideration of his health. If the school has a doctor, he will take on this part of the study. Even without one, though, we can form a picture of the child's state of health. Is this child frequently ill or rarely? If the former is true, what illnesses does he get or has he had? Has he had many accidents, and broken any bones? The child may show us a quite different picture depending on whether he often has a cold or ear infection, or instead has broken a leg or an arm. Chronic or acute diseases reveal a different picture again. The child's health also includes asking how he sleeps. Is his sleep disturbed? Does he find it hard to fall asleep, and to wake up again in the morning?

The pupil's skills and abilities

In relation to this initial picture-forming phase, we have found it helpful to consider his objective achievements and skills or capacities. Let's assume we're talking about a child in Class 3. Here we could ask the following: Can he read and write? How is his spelling? What is his handwriting like? Is it cramped or too loose, well formed or over-formed, or only weakly formed? Handwriting reveals an astonishing amount about a pupil, not only as regards his temperament.

Further questions could concern his counting and maths skills, his drawing and painting. What abilities does he have in foreign languages, in handwork, craft and eurythmy? What does the gymnastics teacher say about him and the music teacher? Alongside the child's spatial and temporal form, a picture of his skills and achievements should also become apparent.

Rounding out the symptomatic picture; refraining from judgements

The three levels of the study gradually condense into a general picture: the child is thus, his appearance is such and such. Having reached this point, we should come back to our initial starting point. What was the reason for considering this child? As general orientation it is very important for all those attending the child study to hear what question the class teacher is living with in relation to the child.

As far as the length of time taken up by this first phase is concerned, it is not at all a bad exercise for the class teacher to try to present the whole thing in quarter of an hour. Rather than impeding his freedom of speech, such concentration has a refreshing effect and is beneficial for the further child study process.

After this presentation, the previously designated chair of the study can then open up the meeting to the group of colleagues who teach the child. It can be useful here to point out that it is unnecessary to repeat things already mentioned that they too have experienced with the child. It is enough to endorse the class teacher's account. Where relevant, the school doctor can add his insights here, if a case history has been recorded or some medical peculiarity has been diagnosed. If the child has suffered a severe illness, for instance, it is worth knowing if he has been to hospital. It is always helpful to mention the age the child was when such a thing occurred.

Here again it is important to note how beneficial it is for the child study process if the picture so far created together is kept 'clean': that is, free of any view or interpretation. It is the task of the faculty or college, and especially of the chair of the child study, to ensure this. In this way the picture of the child is gradually filled and rounded out.

Phenomena and symptoms

During this picture-forming phase, as listeners we can observe something remarkable in ourselves. We listen to the accounts and descriptions of the child, trying to meet all that is said without any personal predilection or opinion. We try to listen so attentively and tangibly that we can feel our way right in to the child's experience. Even if we manage this, we can still note a slight unease in ourselves: Is what I am hearing intrinsic and important for the child, or does it have scarcely any significance for him? Does a particular detail in the description point to something essential in the child or is it only a superficial observation? The account aims to highlight relevant *phenomena* after all. But something stirs in us to seek out descriptions that can make us clairaudient for the riddle of the child. For example, if a hand or voice or stance are described, this *may* have a significance that illumines the riddle of the child. But it does not inevitably do so. As the picture-forming process unfolds, a search is therefore underway for something particular and very specific which we will here call 'symptomatic'. This quiet inner quest for some key that unlocks our understanding of the child can enormously intensify our interest in what is being said.

It is very helpful in this phase of the study to try to relate all the phenomena to each other. For example: Is the child's lack of interest in the teaching content in any way related to the fact his hands are always cold?

This brings us to an important question: What is the difference between the *phenomenon* and the *symptom*? Here is a small example to explain this. Everyone has ears. We look at an ear and see that it belongs to a particular person. The ear is the *phenomenon* here. Then we observe a child's ear more closely, finding that, in this instance, it has a large, rounded arch at the top, with a fine, lightly curved, rounded and extremely well formed middle area, giving a large ear opening. The lower portion of the ear is a little unformed by contrast, as if the 'sculptor' forgot to model it at that point. If we're discussing a pupil who has outstanding intellectual and social skills, but who finds it difficult to engage his will fully, then the ear offers us a vivid picture of this situation. The ear *can* provide a picture of a pupil's overall disposition.

But misunderstandings can easily arise. What this does *not* mean is employing the dire kind of forensic psychology which came to such terrible expression above all in Nazi racial theories: a way of using someone's external physical characteristics to draw conclusions about their inner nature. The example of the ear shows the potentially dangerous aberrations this might lead to. If the shape of the ear is interpreted in line with a certain theory, this will be at odds with the real aim of a child study. In many years as a teacher I have seen just as many ears that were *not* an expression of children's inner *disposition* for particular capacities or qualities as those that were. We need to keep an open mind here. It may be so or it may not. It should not be assumed that a physiological predisposition comes to expression in inner reality. Here's another striking example of the same thing. The relationship between the upper and lower jaw (ideally expressed in a matching 'bite'; the two rows of teeth may however not be properly aligned, or not even come into contact at all) can be regarded as expressing the harmony or otherwise between our upper and lower poles. If the bite matches, our soul-spiritual aspect is thought to be in harmony with etheric and physical. Dentition *can* be a highly significant symptom, but it must be considered in the whole context of observational evidence gathered by subtle processes of perception and thinking. In this process we must seek to preserve the greatest possible intellectual and interpretive clarity, free of any prejudicial colourings of our judgement. Observation of certain bodily and inner qualities should never be governed by classification schemas, let alone by value judgements. Instead, such observation serves to create the fluid, mobile picture of a developing human being. Rather than fixed definitions, we need flexible concepts here that can 'grow alongside' ongoing observation of the child's educational development.

In other words, a symptom offers us a doorway: it gives us *possible* access to understanding the child's being.

We cited the ear as one example, but of course other traits and characteristics can awaken insight. Our search for features potentially characteristic of the child's being, that can help us decipher him, is an outwardly unnoticed activity that occurs in the group of listeners – the whole participating community – during the first part of the child study. This shared search provides the communal strength and foundation for the further discussion, and here listeners are just as active in the process as the teachers who make their presentations.

I'd like to make the following point here. Experience has shown that the first part of the child study can easily exceed its proper scope – scarcely surprising, since this first part is founded on actual experiences of a child, and naturally people are glad to share these.

To get a good grasp on the first part, it is helpful if the teacher in question brings along some work by the pupil. Examination of the child's handwriting, drawings and form drawings, paintings, main lesson books, and handwork, can give good insights into some aspects of his nature. The expressive power of such work can tell us something about the nature of the child's ether body – whether it is vigorous and strong, or weak and poorly formed. Handwriting and handwork should also be considered from the perspective of temperament. What temperament is apparent here? A pupil's paintings reveal an aspect of his inner life or soul. Are they brightly coloured, pale, rich in contrasts, luminous? Here we can sense both a past and a future.

Then some photographs, if possible taken at different ages, can be helpful too in rounding out the picture fully.

At the end of the picture-forming part of the meeting, the chair of the discussion has the task of leading it over into the next phase. This is not always easy, since people generally like dwelling on their perceptions and impressions; these anchor us and can be endlessly extended. However, let it be expressly said here that this first phase does *not* need to be exhaustive. The *overall picture* can in fact surface after only a few, thoughtfully presented accounts and characterizations.

2. Enquiring into causes

At the start of this second phase of the child study, the chairperson will ask what has been learned from the descriptions given, and what insights have been gained.

In this section of the study a tendency will soon become apparent simply to continue characterizing the child; or attempts to answer the above question may even lead to the sharing of further observations from some teachers. However, this will not help us to get any further. It is vital to realize that the picture formed cannot and should not be complete. This is a key insight, for only then can one find a transition to the next step. If there are moments of 'relapse' into the previous, picture-forming stage, the chairperson needs to point out that the presentations of the first part have now been concluded.

A remarkable inner fact arises in this second stage of the child study: one seems to have suddenly lost one's way. We have left behind the safe ground of shared impressions and entered a realm that offers us little outward security: that of *causes*.

At this point it is very important to have the right sense of transition into this entirely new sphere. If discussion becomes halting, accompanied possibly by a feeling of initially inexplicable powerlessness, this is not indicative of a weakness in the faculty. Rather, it marks the transition into a new sphere, requiring quite different capacities and powers of insight. It may happen that silence falls for a moment or two, and that no one seems to have anything to say.

The chairperson can now repeat his initial question. Here the teachers allow themselves the inner space to feel their way into this new domain, gradually sensing the world of causes. Is there anything in what has been described so far that offers any clue to the phenomena? We can note that we're now in very different territory. The rich field of perceptions and impressions has vanished and something quite different is stirring. A teacher may attempt an initial answer, such as the following: 'It's possible that the I organism isn't fully entering the sphere of the senses here, or that it has withdrawn from it somewhat.' (This remark relates to a girl, one of the older children in Class 4, who has suddenly become short-sighted and has therefore started wearing glasses. Since then her interest in everything has faded, and she even appears a little dull-witted, although previously she was thought to be a very lively, cheerful pupil.) This remark sets the stage for other related thoughts from colleagues. Do the descriptions we have heard suggest that we're heading in the right direction with this idea?

The chairperson now has the challenging task of following this thread in the discussion without making it impossible for a different idea to emerge. This requires great sensitivity, since two things can now happen: the proposed idea turns out either to be right or wrong. If it turns out to be mistaken, one or another person will feel called on to suggest another way forward. But how do we know what is 'correct'? The indicator for this is a subtle sense, a feeling or hunch of whether or not one is on the right track. If not, you can suddenly get a feeling that the child is slowly vanishing from view. The discussion then becomes more abstract, and one finds that contact has been lost with an inner reality in which the participants share. This perception does not however necessarily signify a 'mistake' in the child-study process. The important thing is to attend to the subtler processes that only unfold within us, and to a mood that weaves between the colleagues present, being aware of what is happening at any moment. To put it more prosaically, we can also ask this: Is a feeling developing that we are 'on' to something, that evidence is mounting up? Or equally, is it not?

This second stage can quickly lead to an intuition about the child's being as it currently manifests, and an understanding of his reality. Or a longer period of reflection and enquiry may be needed. Sometimes one has to admit, in the end, that the discussion has not reached its goal. No clear picture has arisen, and the attempt will need to be undertaken again in a different meeting. This possibility, however, should not be seen negatively, for it too is a learning experience.

If the child's problems are critical in nature, it may be felt necessary to carry on with the child study at this point. Where no clear picture has arisen in the first stage, we can in fact embark in a different direction.

A further means of discerning causes: studying the child's etheric and soul being

Instead of the path outlined above, there is a surer way

of understanding the developing child. By focusing on the child's apparent *etheric* and *soul* qualities, we can fairly certainly gain understanding of the causes that give rise to the phenomena we have ascertained. In taking this route we find that the picture is more easily differentiated according to individual circumstances. It can be pursued as follows:

In the first part of the study we have developed a picture of the child's appearance, and the way he strikes us. From here a bridge can be built to the second phase of the study, by asking about the child's etheric and soul (astral) configuration. But how do we recognize a person's etheric constitution?

a) The etheric acting within the physical is expressed in everything of a pictorial nature that the child produces:

The following questions can help us discern this level of a child's being:

How does the child draw or paint?
What does his handwriting express?
What is the character of his form drawings?
How does he fill out his main lesson or exercise book?

Observing this work, and especially what it expresses, can awaken an intuitive understanding in us. Is the line well controlled? Is it strong or uncertain? Do the form drawings show that a task has been fully grasped and clearly formed, or does the drawing remain unfocused;

or even unfinished? A child's free drawings also show how formative forces are being mastered. Here we can ask such questions as: Does the drawing express what the child intended? Is there a certain wealth of design in it, or does the picture remain 'thin', only partly realized? How does the pupil use the whole sheet of paper and how does he organize different parts of the picture? Is everything lined up at the bottom, or has he used the whole space? The way a main lesson book is structured can also be expressive of a child's organizing capacities in the pictorial realm.

In all these phenomena we should remember that the temperament also plays a part, and is indeed rooted in the etheric. Then of course the age of the child in question must be taken into consideration in this interpretive stage of the study. Skills and capacities are also linked to the age of a child.

b) The etheric body acting in the sensory realm is expressed in capacities of memory and thought, the ability to think in general, and the grasping of ideas.
Steiner is quite precise when he calls the etheric body the 'learning body'. At a later stage in the child study we will see that this is a very helpful idea. We observe this realm not in order to assess the child's intelligence, but to study how the capacities of intelligence, as an expression of the etheric body, find their way into the physical body. Here our attention focuses on *learning achievements*. What does the child accomplish in this domain at school or also at home? Can he read well, how are his maths skills, his ability in foreign lan-

guages, his capacities of memory? What is the impression we form of the pupil here, the inner picture we gain? This has nothing to do with the superficial question of whether a pupil is 'weak' or 'strong'. Instead we try to pursue the deeper question of how his neuro-sensory life is nourished by the etheric forces.

Next we ask how the soul or psyche (the astral body) lives and expresses itself in corporeality.

c) The soul (one can also say the sentient body or – in a nutshell – the astral body) is expressed in all speech, colour and musical-rhythmic qualities:
To grasp this level it is, for instance, helpful to study a child's wet-in-wet paintings (especially if they contain no figurative forms, but only colour compositions). Here we can ask:

How does the child live in colours?
What comes to expression here?
Can the child use colours to convey something specific?
Or is there a sense of randomness?

One should also 'hearken' to the pupil's voice. How does he speak? What tone does his voice have? Does he speak melodiously? Is his voice high or low? Is the voice pleasant to listen to or rough and hoarse? All these things indicate a 'picture' of how the soul lives in the body.

Singing too deserves attention. The very fact that a child can sing uninhibitedly, or join in singing with others, says something about the relationship of soul and body. If a child doesn't want to sing, or is unable to, perhaps even refuses, this should give us pause for thought. Usually this is not indicative of 'unwillingness' but almost always of some blockage in the soul's expression.

d) Eurythmy gives visible expression to the soul.
Eurythmy seeks not only to gesture physically but also to lend this gesture a soul-spiritual expressiveness. The soul itself sends this inner gesture into the body's movements. In this sphere we find, therefore, not just an interior sentience but the expression of a communicating quality of soul. Nowadays children increasingly find it hard to communicate their inner life through gestures; and therefore eurythmy, given originally as a way to help the soul communicate, is needed more than ever.

Some children take to eurythmy – as to singing for example – very naturally. This too tells us something about how 'available' the soul is to come to physical expression. Others find it a challenge, and feel 'embarrassed'. If such pupils avoid imparting expression to these gestures, or are unable to do this, it indicates that they are as yet unable to properly incorporate the corresponding aspect of soul. Once again, this is not 'unwillingness'.

In child studies sometimes, teachers report that a child 'does not (want to) look at the teacher' when greeting him in the morning; or that he becomes uncommunicative if he has done something wrong, refusing to admit his action or withdrawing into himself entirely. On other occasions, likewise, one can observe children who, when told off, say they know nothing about the deed in question, or have no idea whether they have done it or not. They may certainly have been present, but none of them seem to know who actually 'did it'.

Such examples show us that something is not (yet) properly connecting in the relationship between I and soul on the one hand, and the etheric and physical on the other. In such instances one should avoid making moral judgements. A child really cannot – usually – be blamed for such (lack of) relationship, which is due to his constitution. The only thing that can help here is the more roundabout approach of creating a therapeutic story which conveys a picture of what has occurred, and telling it to the class. Directly addressing the issue with the child has no point in this case.

In summary we can ascertain that by forming a picture of the child's etheric and soul configuration, we will succeed in finding our way into the second part of the child study.

The need for a different quality of thinking in the second stage

Above we described the three stages of the child study as: forming a picture, then seeking the causes, and thirdly, giving help. We can also say that the first stage draws primarily on *pictorial thinking*, while the second requires a *feeling thinking* or *thinking feeling*, and is far more delicate and subtle in nature. The child study participants also need a certain courage to embark on this second phase, since here we enter a realm of non-sensory realities.

If we are to understand the child's being, we need to equip ourselves with faculties drawn from 'beyond the threshold' of the sensory world. We need to remember this continually whenever we speak of the child's different 'bodies': ether body, sentient body, sentient soul, astral body and so forth. If we lose our awareness of this other sphere, our feeling for non-sensory realities and levels, our conversation about the child will focus on him as on a 'thing'. The discussion will become superficial and crass. We will not succeed in approaching the child's being, which will then withdraw from us.

It is not easy to characterize this subtle and sensitive process. In the second stage of the child study, thinking must lose its 'angularity'. We should try to bring mobility, fluidity and openness into our thinking. For example, if in this stage of the study one has a different opinion from that of a colleague, and directly expresses this supposed error, believing it necessary to correct it, one destroys the fine, sensitive interweaving of thoughts. A first step towards mobility of thinking, in fact, is *allowing different thoughts to live alongside each other*. The inner dynamic of the discussion, and of truly involved colleagues, will ensure that appropriate findings arise. (Whether we 'just' think that our colleague is wrong, or also express this in words makes little difference. It is important to be aware that the negative effect is exactly the same.)

Thus the child study develops and employs a culture of discussion that makes different demands on our thinking, listening, silence and speaking than is the case in 'normal' dialogue:

- In our *thinking* we try to stay fully present and attentive. We can try to keep wandering thoughts firmly in check. The better we manage this, in fact, the more likely it is that good ideas will surface.
- In our *listening* it is important to switch off (and not just turn down the volume of) our inner 'commentator' or 'radio': in other words, not to meet what we hear with our own opinions and judgements. It can help if we really try to sense what someone is trying to say, even if he doesn't find the best words or formulations. I have often heard of teachers who no longer speak up in meetings because of all the never-ending 'radio waves'. It makes no difference whether these are audible or not. If such anxieties become embedded in the culture of a faculty meeting, the school has a problem, and it will be difficult to hold child studies at all. A form of work as sensitive as this can only be realized if peace reigns in the college's social fabric.
- *Being silent* in the right way is also an art. We all know what it feels like when someone says nothing because he has long since inwardly withdrawn, but carries on dutifully sitting there. It is a quite different experience if someone says nothing but you

feel he is fully present. You can participate without saying anything. In fact, it is precisely this stance which makes the group a real one, for, after all, not everybody can speak at once.

— What can we practise when *speaking*? We can for instance try to sense when the right moment has arrived for our own contribution. Will it help the process if I say something now? Or has my speaking become a kind of reflex habit I give way to without even knowing whether I have anything significant to say or not? It is worth practising a certain reticence here. I may even have found that the right measures were discovered without my own opinion being uttered.

Here a further remark is necessary. In this second phase of the meeting, a kind of *associative psychologising* can arise. For example: The child is so withdrawn because his aunt is depressive. The girl is mad about horses because she gets no love at home. The boy can't concentrate because his grandmother has died, etc. etc. Such reductive 'insights' are of little value and usually lead nowhere. There is no real basis for these conjectures, and they have no reality. Grandmothers always die, and being mad about horses is quite normal in girls at a certain age. Yet our waking consciousness loves these causal associations, since they arise so easily but can also seem original.

It certainly isn't easy to capture in words the subtle observations and perceptions at work in this phase of the study. A colleague may suddenly have a genuinely helpful thought which gives insight into the nature of the child. But one has to learn to perceive such things. At this stage, everything depends on fine subtleties.

Where do we focus our attention in the second stage?

We can only perceive something if we already have within us the idea of the object of perception. Otherwise we see nothing. The Latin root of the word 'perceive' encompasses the idea of 'taking possession', which is something we can only do by finding the idea 'realized' before us in the act of seeing, thus making a reality our own.

A child study will get nowhere if the faculty group has not in some way – whether individually or as a community of teachers – acquired thought pictures or concepts that give them a capacity to 'see' or recognize the nature of the human being in some way. Such pictures are of significant help in this second stage. The child we are considering will only become fully real to us if we recognize his distinctive nature and thus learn to understand his being.

Thought pictures or concepts of this kind might include:

- the picture of the temperaments
- the picture of the threefold human being (upper, middle and lower systems)
- the picture of the fourfold human being (physical, etheric, astral and I)

- modes of human thinking (or also whether someone has a 'small-' or 'large-headed' disposition)
- the child's capacity for imagination (present or not, dominant?)
- a pupil's focus of interest (more cosmic [idealistic] or more prosaic [earthly]?)
- the picture of the self or the I in relation to the body (too loose a connection or too rooted in the body?)
- behavioural disturbances such as ADHD, autism, anorexia. (Here though one must be very careful; while such terminology is very diverse, it can often constrain the flow of thoughts in the child study, and inhibit or even check it altogether.)
- learning disabilities such as dyslexia or dyscalculia (again beware of rigidity arising from these terms)

Such pictures can be augmented by the overall impression one gains of the child: does this convey brightness, alertness and coolness or does it instead seem dark and warm? This 'picture' can help us grasp children who have been unusually awake from an early age, or in other words show an alert awareness, without them necessarily being 'intellectual'.

Addictive behaviour, increasingly common in young people today, is really a subject in itself. This includes computer games, unchecked involvement in social media – which teachers too can suffer from – and excessive media consumption in general; or also substance addictions (alcohol, drugs of all kinds). If this problem surfaces in a child study, it must of course be included in the picture. At the same time however, we should remember that the whole climate in the school, and its whole social context, will play a part here. This is why the theme of addiction can easily exceed the scope of a child study, and therefore it is a good idea to set up a discussion forum devoted to this issue. Here the school can (and no doubt ought to) commission a small group of colleagues to take responsibility for this field and report back to the larger group on its findings.

Experience has shown that the above 'tools' – as long as they are used in a flexible and individualized way rather than as stereotype definitions – enable us to understand more or less all phenomena that children nowadays display.

The process involved here makes clear why child studies should not draw on checklists and programmatic procedures, which can predetermine the outcome rather than allowing real, new insights into the child whom one desires to help.

In practising this art of the child study as here described, one increasingly finds that the pupil himself shows us the methodology we need. The child himself, rather than a predetermined agenda, actually governs and directs our thoughts. If we succeed in working 'cleanly' in this way and reining in our haste to interpret things, we can find ourselves in a state that could, metaphorically, be described as 'hearing' what wants to be said.

It would be quite accurate to see this way of working as a powerful exercise in mobile, living thinking. In this field of work, all definitions are an injury to the unfolding process and thus also do injury to the child who is being discussed. If we set off in a wrong direction during the discussion, we notice that our growing understanding of the child fades from us again, and we are further from our goal. Then a new effort is needed to find our way back to the right way of working.

In the second stage of the child study, the child's underlying temperament (as an aspect of the etheric realm) should not be overlooked.

The child's temperament and daily school life

Those who find the theme of temperaments problematic can try approaching it in terms of a polarity between *inner strength* and *sensitivity*.[20] To gain a better grasp of temperament we can ask whether a pupil lives more out of himself, i.e. from within outwards, or is he 'informed' more by his experiences, thus living from outside inwards. In the first case the temperament is more choleric (melancholic); in the second, more sanguine (phlegmatic). The child's build too – whether he seems tall and thin or compact and 'compressed', and likewise the gesture of his movements, can help us decide the temperament. Here it's useful to observe a games or gym lesson. If you are still getting nowhere, the following suggestion can help: Steiner describes the temperament as an 'intermediate' factor between the upper and lower poles. From this perspective in particular, the temperament plays a much more important role than we tend to think. It's worth considering the following comment by Steiner:

The moment one can properly judge a child's temperament, everything else will follow naturally. One ought really to acquire such a clear sense of it that, in calling the child's name, one already conveys his temperament in one's tone of voice.[21]

Reflecting on this statement, we can ask ourselves what Steiner intended when he introduced the temperaments into Waldorf pedagogy. For some teachers, and for educationalists in general, they remain a bone of contention, often sadly with good reason.

It was as far as possible from Steiner's intentions that the temperaments should be used as some kind of 'label' to pigeonhole children.

Nor was he merely reviving an antiquated doctrine of the humours as taught by Galen of Pergamon (a teaching retained to this day in some old sayings and phrases). Rather, he proposed the temperaments as a bridge of understanding between pupils and teachers. A child has a deep, unexpressed need to be recognized and understood by his teachers. If I say to a melancholic girl in Class 4, 'Oh come on, cheer up!' she almost certainly won't. It is likely that she'll do the opposite in fact. But if I tell her confidentially that I came to school today even though I have a bad headache, such a child can respond by feeling inwardly warmer and happier.*

Here's another example, this time relating to the phlegmatic temperament. A teacher had a very phlegmatic girl in her class. In a class play, she gave the girl

---

* Translator's note: This must however of course be true!

the role of standing on stage throughout, depicting a tree. Some teachers thought she had gone too far with this. But later, when she was grown-up, she reported how very happy she had been to be involved without being required to do anything.

It's great to discuss the weekend's football results with the boys in Class 5 or 6 – just briefly and easily, but with some interest and knowledge! It's over and done within five minutes.

It may seem as if, in respect for the individual freedom of future teaching colleagues, Steiner did not wish the temperaments to be seen as a tool of self-education. And yet effective use of the temperaments in education only comes about if the teacher is, on the one hand, able to identify his pupils' temperaments, and on the other to get a grip on his own temperament fully enough to respond to their temperaments and actively intervene in this way in situations. A child or adolescent whose temperamental nuance the teacher addresses in a tactful and discreet way, will feel that the teacher understands him.

The temperaments are based on a fundamental polarity. Each temperament consists of a corresponding blend of the two aspects of this polarity, which is also that of human existence itself: sensitivity and receptivity for what approaches us, on the one hand, and on the other, inner strength. In other words, the world approaches me, and I go to meet the world.

The phlegmatic temperament displays a certain tranquillity in both directions.

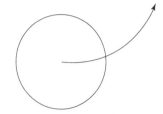

Sensitivity to what affects
us from without

Inner strength: I reveal myself
to the world

The sanguine temperament, by contrast, shows great sensitivity to what approaches from without, but responds relatively weakly from within.

The melancholic temperament, on the other hand, has plenty of inner energy, but does not easily connect this with external experiences, preferring in a sense to dwell within itself.

The choleric temperament, finally, is highly sensitive but at the same time shows strong inner involvement.

It is clear what Steiner is aiming for in his description of the temperaments and his pedagogical suggestions: Do we educate in a way that reinforces the children *as* their temperaments, or, instead, so that we ourselves and thus the children and pupils also, *own* or *possess* the temperament? In other words, does our temperament become a one-sided characteristic or instead can it offer us the potential to act, in the sense of a skill or quality at our disposal. In his observations, Steiner invariably is concerned with practice rather than theory.

But if the temperament becomes a burdensome,
one-sided characteristic,
the phlegmatic remains a lazybones,
the sanguine a scatterbrain,
the melancholic self-centred, and
the choleric a tyrant.

Then one *is* one's temperament: it fuses with us as it were. If, on the other hand, we transform it by learning to handle or play it like an instrument – taking our basic temperament and shaping it – then a different picture arises, which we can describe thus: the temperament becomes potential instead of remaining a hindrance. And then
the phlegmatic develops the virtue of loyalty,
the sanguine the virtue of interest,
the melancholic the virtue of empathy,
of compassion,
the choleric the virtue of creative initiative.

Yet these virtues are available to everyone. In this way, the temperament becomes modified by each virtue into generally human potential.

Another intransigent misunderstanding relates to the way temperaments themselves develop. We have already indicated the remarkable nature of our temperament – that we can both *have* it and *be* it. But this does not exclude the possibility of transformative processes between the two.

As we grow older the temperaments change. A

young businessman, scarcely out of puberty, has something choleric and tumultuous about him. At this age we all want to improve or conquer the world to some degree. This cools noticeably as we reach middle age and realize we have failed to achieve all we wished to. In reflective people at least, this can lead to a certain disillusionment. Much has not happened as I envisaged. The evening of our life often brings with it more serenity: all in all, things were good as they were – a contrast with the sunny stance of youth with its desire to drink life to the full. In this serenity we see a more phlegmatic tinge colouring the individual temperament.

Yet a single temperament seldom appears in isolation. In almost all children, the predominant temperament is mixed with another: one coming to the fore more strongly while the other is secondary. We can think of this in musical terms, as dominant and subdominant. A predominantly melancholic child with choleric as subdominant can change at puberty into a predominantly choleric adolescent.

A phlegmatic child can change after puberty into a more sanguine person. During puberty no adolescent stays the way they used to be. As teachers we have the task here of proper perception, proper observation: of really getting to know the young person, accompanying him with our attentive and loving interest. The child and adolescent are in a state of development, changing continually.

In relation to health issues it is also important to mention how the temperament is connected with the threefold human being. When the temperaments are not reined in, they can also lapse into pathological behaviour. One sometimes hears of students doing class observation in Waldorf schools who regularly witness (usually male) teachers raging and shouting in front of their class, or (usually female) teachers crying in front of their pupils because lessons aren't going well. Quite apart from the lack of professionalism in this behaviour, this also shows that the teacher in question has not got a grip on his temperament. At such a moment one has *become* one's temperament, and this will invariably lead to a rude awakening.[22]

In relation to the threefold human being, Steiner states that the melancholic temperament is rooted in the neuro-sensory system, the choleric temperament in the metabolism, and that *both* the sanguine and phlegmatic temperament are rooted in the rhythmic system. He makes a brief supplementary remark here: the two latter, he says, are therefore in principle more healthy, while the melancholic and choleric temperament can, as the examples show, easily become diverted into unhealthy channels.

In conclusion let us consider the long-term repercussions for health of exposure to a decidedly one-sided temperament. It is however also worth studying the primary literature on this subject.[23]

If a class-teacher erupts in anger once a year, that is regrettable but won't harm the pupils. It is different if the rage erupts once a week. This will call forth a harmful response in the very sensitive nature of the child or adolescent. An outbreak of fury and shouting always evokes fear in pupils. What happens when this is regularly repeated? As we know fear enters our limbs and doesn't remain a perception at a cognitive level only. Since Steiner was interested above all in the life-long effects of education, he studied this phenomenon with the means at his disposal, and came to the following conclusion: repeated experiences of alarm can lead, as long-term effect, to a weakening and therefore a susceptibility of the rhythmic system (manifesting for instance in cardiac insufficiency and heart disorders) in the 'second half of life'.

Steiner studies such effects further, perceiving how lasting exposure to another person's one-sided temperament causes dispositions for certain diseases. For example, the lasting influence of an unconstrained melancholic temperament will lead to a predisposition for metabolic disorders. If pupils are by contrast exposed to a sanguine temperament that the adult does not get a grip on, this will lead to lack of vitality; and, if a teacher is too phlegmatic, to a susceptibility to nervous problems.

It is important to remember that we're speaking of long-term effects here. This kind of predisposition will usually only become apparent in the second half of life. At one point Steiner even shows how the effects can be precisely calculated.

It is therefore understandable that current research on former Waldorf pupils seeks ways to trace this phenomenon. In 2012, Dr. Christopher Hueck published a study* on the health of former Waldorf pupils as compared with a non-Waldorf control group.

(It should also be mentioned here that in the faculty

meeting of 14 June 1920 – CW 300a – Steiner gave important suggestions for understanding the connection between temperament and zodiac constellation.)

In the second part of the child study, our gaze can broaden to encompass the mode of thinking which we perceive in the child. Is it basically more analytic or synthetic in nature? This can be important for any proposed pedagogical measures. When considering this domain, we can also observe a possible correlation between the child's mode of thinking and the physical shape of his head. But the following must of course be stated: deciding whether a child is 'small-' or 'large-headed' should be seen in a much broader context than is generally assumed, and it is precisely this context that is important for the child study.[24] Here too I would like to refer to a key passage in a lecture by Steiner. On 6 February 1923, he first speaks at length about 'educational health measures', relating to the distinctive configuration of each child's threefold nature. This 'distinctive mix' requires a pedagogical approach from the teacher. Learning to perceive and balance the child's constitution, he can thus nurture the child's health.

It is particularly important, above all, that our whole conduct within the school in relation to chil-

* Hueck et al.: 'The Effect of Attending Steiner Schools during Childhood on Health in Adulthood: A Multicentre Cross-Sectional Study'.

dren's health is informed by the teacher's full grasp of the threefold human organism. This has to live in his flesh and blood if you like. In relation to every child the teacher should have an instinctive sense of whether the activity of one or another system predominates: the neurosensory system, the rhythmic system or the system of metabolism and limbs; and whether, we need to rebalance a harmful predominance of one system by stimulating the activity of another.[25]

Large- and small-headedness need to be considered from this perspective. The shape of the head itself is not the prime issue here, since this is only an indicator of any observed one-sidedness. The key observation is whether the child's thinking has a fleeting, flitting, inattentive quality ('one could also say, too sanguine or phlegmatic') in which case we will have a large-headed child before us. Such children rest in themselves, whatever may be going on around them. And we can have a sense, arising from this predisposition, that they are not learning anything!

The opposite picture is found in children who live within themselves (meaning that they do not easily and naturally connect with their surroundings). They are irritated by outer impressions because they react too strongly to what is happening around them. In a sense they are too exposed to what is happening in the class, since the system of metabolism and limbs does not act strongly enough in their head. These 'small-headed' children easily become nervous and are quickly drawn into situations they actually do not want to be in at all.

Since the context of Rudolf Steiner's remarks is the general health of children, in the first instance he suggests a salty diet, and in the second one that is sweeter. Astonishingly, he does not propose any educational measures as such to deal with this problem, but suggests only a dietary solution – an example of how very diverse Steiner's pedagogical measures are.

And so, in the second part of the child study we also ask how the neuro-sensory system, the rhythmic system and the system of limbs and metabolism relate to each other in this particular child. What specific picture do we have here? By proceeding in this observational way, we can come a little closer to the riddle that each child or adolescent presents us with. But it is vital to remember and repeatedly remind ourselves that we are *never* dealing with distinct and separate picture here. We will return to this theme a little later.

At this point in the study we can ask ourselves whether the riddle of the child is beginning to disclose itself to us, or whether it still remains concealed. How do we get further? Let us enquire into the child's powers *of thinking, picturing and imagining*. Let us ask how he *stands between heaven and earth*. How does he express his *inclinations and interests*? How does his *identity or entelechy relate to his corporeality*? Do we experience *heaviness* not only in his physicality, but also in the way *his soul expresses itself*? Or is everything (too) *light*: nothing of much importance, everything simply the way life presents it?

In the second part of the child study we can also try to find a picture or metaphor for what *cannot yet* be precisely identified. Pictures drawn from nature are helpful. And it is important to attend to whether such images arise from realms of nature that are lifeless, living or sentient. (For instance, the hedgehog conveys a different moral stance on the part of the speaker than that of a concrete bunker.)

Another approach involves imagining oneself into the child, asking how it feels to be in his skin, either in the sense of his bodily experience or intuiting how his behaviour feels to him. What does it feel like, for instance, never to be able to sit still? Or never be able to express himself?

Anyone who has attempted to feel or imagine their way into another's mode of being, will quickly gain an existential sense that what we experience outwardly in the other as being at odds with us, a nuisance, is something that the person concerned *cannot help doing*. An example can show exactly what this means: a boy in Class 5 bumps into other, usually younger children at playtime, and hurts them. He isn't doing this intentionally, but may be so 'stuck in his head', i.e. so poorly connected with the rest of his body, that this is his way of making contact with other children. And when he is told off, one often finds that he isn't really aware of what he has done. He's not pretending, but really can't help it. And this is something we have to acknowledge, without moral judgement.

A further example: a boy who can draw trams and aeroplanes down to every last detail, or a girl who can draw caricatures to perfection. Yet astonishingly, neither is able to manage a form drawing or other drawing task. They are not unwilling, lazy or even 'inartistic' or 'weak-willed'. No, they just can't help it. And they can't because they are gifted in a limited field that cannot be communicated in any other way. Their capacity does not relate to a gift for drawing but is an expression of having fixed ideas stuck within an image complex. This is why they have to keep on drawing the same motifs, and are, in a sense, plagued by this ability.

When speaking of waking and sleeping consciousness, Steiner uses other words to describe the capacity for entering children's reality and experiencing it from within, which is often called 'empathy' (a term coined by the great humanistic psychologist Carl Rogers). Our capacity for empathy enables us to enter in a dreamy, feeling way into another being, as if sleeping into them; and then, on awakening again from them, to return with the gift of an intuition.

This sharpens our awareness of what happens in the second part of the child study. The process can be clarified in a simple diagram, in which the direction of the arrows is of great importance. These depict what occurs in full wakefulness (allowing of course for the fact that we are not always 'awake' when we're awake).

(Otto Scharmer, in his well-regarded work entitled 'Theory U', also largely bases his U procedure on this principle: all understanding of contexts other than the merely physical and mechanical passes from thinking cognizance through feeling to will. This also holds true

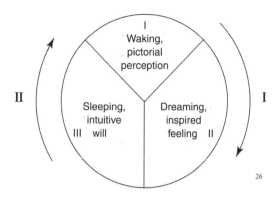

I Waking, pictorial perception

II Dreaming, inspired feeling

III Sleeping, intuitive will

II

I

26

if will reveals itself to thought in intuition. [Arrow II in the drawing returns to the beginning of the process.])[27]

3. Finding helpful measures

If the child study has successfully illumined a sense of the child's true being, so that the causes of his idiosyncrasies have at least begun to be understood, the chair of the meeting can then ask what measures are needed to help the child.

Sometimes, simply due to the urgency of the situation, ways of helping must still be sought even before the dawning of full insight or understanding. This is also a possibility.

Nevertheless, one should at least have attempted the second stage, that of seeking underlying causes, in order to avoid a merely superficial combating of symptoms (e.g., a lad in Class 10 has done this or that, and therefore he needs this punishment or therapy).

In approaching this third part of the child study, a further uncertainty can arise, similar to that experienced in the second stage. How shall we continue now? What is the next step? What needs to happen?

At this point the chairperson can ask: How can we help this child? Or: What shall we do? People may initially make further contributions that are still to do with the previous stage, the second phase of the study. But those listening can already hear that another stance is necessary to move on to the next step.

Whereas we need courage in the second stage in pursuing an idea and testing, in way more related to inspiration, whether this idea is equal to the reality of the circumstances, the will is now invoked. How can we help? Involvement is necessary, and commitment: a sense of engaging with the question of what might really aid the child and bring him further. Here the *creative pedagogical will to help* is needed.

The basis for finding appropriate means of help

Before considering the process involved here itself, we will preface this with a few perspectives that form an important basis for the third part of the study.

The need to develop pedagogical insights

Just as, when a child is to be punished for something, teachers are urged not to punish the pupil as such but his action, so we now need to find something that offers the child the right kind of help in realizing our range of pedagogical insights. For example, giving a child the task of watering the plants in the classroom regularly, or caring for a guinea-pig, are actions with *very* limited scope. The real kind of help we need to find involves pedagogical measures.

This is the realm of *effective imponderables*. Here's one example: a student in Class 11, incredibly skilled at getting up to (sometimes) very inventive mischief, and brilliant at playing the innocent the moment he is caught, is discussed by his upper school teachers. Basically he's thought to be a good student, though one with a fairly unbridled sanguine temperament inhabiting a pretty ungoverned astral body. The biology teacher suggests getting the young man to do a project on the chameleon, and presenting this to the class. The task is given and accomplished to the satisfaction of all concerned. After this, the teachers start to notice a gradual but marked change in the student's behaviour. His former crazy and random actions calm down, he becomes more thoughtful, and an initially tentative but ever-growing sense of his aims and goals becomes apparent. Later asked about these occurrences when grown up, he explains that this project on the chameleon led him to question his behaviour for the first time and who he actually was.

Another example: a boy in Class 4 simply cannot concentrate on his schoolwork. Everything going on around him is just too interesting. His work is far below expectations, but in the child study the teachers agree that he isn't stupid, though his writing and maths are very poor. Instead of plaguing the boy with further exhortations, a teacher suggests that at the end of main lesson, or at the end of the school day, he recapitulate to the class what has happened during that lesson or day. This is a mildly taxing way of internalizing events. The teachers do in fact succeed in implementing this measure, and quicker than expected the boy starts to work in a concentrated fashion.

One last example: a girl in Class 5, slim, blond and light. She always has cold hands. She certainly is not stupid, but her ability to learn is very limited. She is very preoccupied with appearance and fashion. Tirelessly she draws one fashion model after another, always to a fixed schema, as if her world consists of this alone. In the child study someone suggests it would be essential for her to draw other things; but it is reported that she has no desire at all to draw or paint other motifs, such as a landscape in Geography. When she has to do this, she seems very 'unskilled' and all her ability at drawing the fashion models evaporates. And so another suggestion is made. It is decided that in the next grammar main lesson, which in Class 5 will fortunately deal with the accusative and dative cases, the teacher should take all his examples from the world of fashion and clothing. This was strikingly successful: for the first time the girl really paid attention and participated in the lessons, and the grammar exercises gave her a new engagement with learning.

These small examples can tell us three things.

Firstly that the most effective pedagogical measures come from curriculum subjects themselves.

Secondly, that measures usually work better if they are indirect. Poor maths is not necessarily improved by doing more maths. A preoccupation with externalities will not become less through prohibition but rather by taking this externality into a more inward activity, as it were including and taking account of it. And a one-sided disposition in a child's developing character is not healed by confrontation but by a loving and sometimes also mildly humorous picture.

Thirdly, for such things to succeed, teachers have to undertake to *really carry out* an agreed measure. Experience has shown that it is precisely this need for implementation that makes teachers tentative or hesitant.

In summary, the third stage of the child study requires this creative pleasure in discovering what will help the child in question, hopefully in the long term.

In a sense you can say that in this third part demand is placed less on the teachers' knowledge and insight than on their will to help the child.

As we will see, in difficult cases it is essential that the faculty of teachers acquires a thorough knowledge of the effect of curriculum subjects on the different levels of the growing child's being, for this is where the most important aids can be found.

Is there a role for parents in the child study?

It is perfectly possible to involve parents in a child study, and to ask them, if they wish, to help shape it. There is no objection in *principle*. But nor is it right simply to state that parents ought to be there. This is something that needs to be carefully considered.

How is the school's overall relationship with the parents? Does it generally cultivate trusting interactions with parents? What is the quality of collaboration between class-teachers and parents? Is there an open, supportive relationship? Is it possible to broach any difficulties with each other? Or are there (often unspoken) tensions? Is it necessary for a teacher new to the profession who is holding his first child study to invite the parents? It can be helpful, or also sometimes a hindrance. Everything depends here on his and his colleagues' sense of tact.

Even if one doesn't ask the parents to attend, it is still right to tell them about it. The class-teacher can then have a conversation with them in which he explains why he needs the help of his colleagues to address a problem he cannot resolve alone. And the parents can perhaps help by providing information. In this case, the *outcome* of the child study should also always be communicated to them.

The most important thing overall however is this: *The tone of the child study should always be maintained as if the child himself or his parents were present. Only then will it have positive results.*

This leads to a last important point. It will sometimes be necessary to say something about the child's home life in a child study. This can be necessary to arrive at a full understanding of the pupil. Relevant themes might include: what is the family configuration: are there younger or older siblings? Are the parents divorced? Is the mother ill or the father absent? Has the family moved a great deal? And so on. Such information must be treated with the greatest reticence and confidentiality. One should as far as possible avoid pat expressions which might come over as in any way judgmental, such as 'single mother'. Such mothers already have enough to deal with. The parental home must never be held responsible for the problems which *we* have. For the same reason one should be extremely cautious about making suggestions to parents in relation to things that will help the child at school, which is the task of teachers. The parents are not substitute teaching assistants. This stance creeps in before one is aware of it. In reality it usually originates in a professional deficiency rather than the kind of quality awareness that a Waldorf school should subscribe to.

What is normal development?
The 'ideal child'

In seeking helpful measures we always need to try to clarify what our view of *normal development* is. But here two problems inevitably arise.

In a more theoretical, not fully living view of anthroposophically oriented anthropology, an unintended, semi-conscious and unspoken idea of what a child *ought to be* can easily arise. A child 'ought' to correspond to all our ideals of childhood. Anything not *like this* becomes a 'problem'. In schools therefore, you often see an educational and social division into 'easy' and 'difficult' children. This is a stance that must be overcome wherever it emerges. The only viable standard is to *take the child as he or she is, and work with it.*

How do we overcome this stereotype picture of a child that we form more or less unconsciously? Here again, Steiner embarks in a quite different direction in his recommendations to teachers.

As such, it is a wonderful quality in a teacher to have an ideal and take his lead from it. This is miles better than the flat realism one can sometimes perceive in teachers' stance towards pupils. But we need the right scope and place for bringing such ideals to life.

Firstly, a general remark about ideals in general: even Steiner's seven-year rhythms of development do not precisely accord with reality but with a developmental ideal. We only become fully human when these human biographical rhythms surface in our life so that we gradually approach the human archetype.

No doubt this is why Steiner points out in the first lecture of *Practical Advice to Teachers* that a great many children who get into difficulties in mainstream education may arrive at the Waldorf school. This is a destiny we ought not to object to. In other words, we get 'difficult' children, and many pupils who come to us late. I would now like to reproduce the whole passage in which this remark figures. What Steiner says there is something that can be seen as a serious and important question which we can repeatedly consider. Let us sense what Steiner is *trying* to say here? We can certainly notice that he is struggling to find the right words to express what he wants to say:

> I will now say something unusual, but if we wish to be educators in the real sense we need to bring alive in us the principles of human nature. There are exceptions, where someone can catch up on something he missed out earlier in his life. To do so he will need to suffer a grave illness, or other such wrenching of his nature – have broken a leg, say, that has never fully set in the right position; in other words, his etheric body must have detached itself from the physical body in some way. Naturally this is risky. If it occurs through karma, it just has to be accepted. But we can't count on such things, or lay down any rules in general for catching up in this way on a stage of development that has been missed, let alone for other things. Human development is a mysterious thing, and what teaching and education must endeavour to do *should never be based on abnormality, but always only on normality. For this reason teaching is always a social activity. For this reason we should always ask what the right age is for developing certain powers so that these can lead a person into life in the right way. We therefore have to count on the fact that certain abilities that people need in order to survive what life throws at them, can only develop in them between the ages of 7 and 14* (author's emphasis).[28]

From this account by Steiner we can definitely perceive that ideals are *essential* to education. One must inevitably develop these ideals from such ideas, and the human being himself is the standard according to which we form these ideals.

In this way we can also see why many teachers strive to form a certain ideal picture of the child or pupil. But it is also necessary to practise clear discernment here, and *allow pedagogical tact to prevail*. An ideal should never mean that we impose a fixed schema on a whole class community, but rather should seek in each individual child for what can help him to accord most fully with his own being and grow into his own humanity.

Fields of responsibility and professional help

Increasing specialization in pedagogical and psychological disciplines today means that development regarded as normal until quite recently is today seen as problematic. Accordingly, specialized provision is offered. These facts require teachers to find a new relationship to their domain of responsibility. They need to ask whether they wish to be 'fully' responsible or whether responsibilities are shared or also sometimes 'outsourced'. In other words, pedagogical and therapeutic measures are handed over to specialists. It is very well worth discussing in a faculty meeting whether this is likely to lead to appropriate pedagogical practice. Today, the scope of 'normality' has become very narrow. Nevertheless, according to paediatricians, 96 percent of development is still within the normal range.[29]

This high degree of regularity within normal development is a fact we can take to heart, and can also be cited in parents' evenings. Running counter to it, though, is another fact: that our modern society in the 21st century subscribes to a typical ideal of childhood – not the idea of the growing human being developing towards his intrinsic archetype but a more functional picture. We strive for perfect pupils: intelligent, athletic, social and with good exam results. This superficial, functional picture is one the mainstream has dedicated itself to in the supposition that acquiring culture and education is feasible – which of course it is to a certain degree. The question is only what ideal picture we are striving for in the educational process. But 'feasibility thinking' has a cost. If a child does not develop in a way that corresponds to the ideal, people no longer look to teachers but to specialists. And here we must ask what our stance and conduct should be.

Outwardly determined criteria for development give rise to problematic developmental scenarios which cause a lot of anxiety today. Such criteria, with their attendant problematization, used not to exist to the same extent.

Thus we must ask what the archetype of a school should be. Is it still enough to have a school doctor, a eurythmy therapist, perhaps art therapists and a 'support class'? When do we need external professional help? It is hard to say. If it is decided that psychiatric help is needed, or that a child has a genuine medical problem (if the school does not have a doctor, as is usually the case), one should avoid thinking one 'knows best' and can do whatever is needed, but must immediately seek the required help. But what about educational and behavioural problems? There we are usually better placed than specialists who come in from outside. We can do a great deal to support children with dyslexia, dyscalculia, hyperactivity, learning difficulties and behavioural problems if we use the child study as a regular part of faculty meetings, and if we develop our skills as creative pedagogues. The child study commonly also has an enlivening effect on those who attend it and the whole school.

Social classes with a closer, or more problematic, relationship to education; and general childhood and adolescent health

We must also be aware that illnesses in childhood and youth are in general shifting from acute to chronic conditions. The results of the nationwide survey in Germany – the 'Child and Adolescent Survey' (KIGGS 2003–2006, which studied 17 641 participants) showed that children in Germany can no longer be certain of growing up to enjoy mental or emotional health.[30] This is cause for concern, and has unmistakable consequences for education.

Finally it should be noted that social divisions are increasing, i.e. that parts of the population with little affinity for education experience more problems of this nature than the 'middle classes'. Since most Waldorf pupils come from middle-class backgrounds, the majority of them are healthy by these standards.[31]

These factors apply in Germany and the industrialized nations. With one exception: the intercultural Waldorf School in Mannheim draws its pupils from disadvantaged backgrounds, and is also located in a socially deprived area. The school has been the subject of outcome research since it was founded, and we therefore already know that it has proven its worth as a school. Social and language integration is far above the average for comparable schools. It is interesting that this school has adhered especially to the originating ideas of the Waldorf school, and is therefore *more* of one than many traditional Waldorf schools.

Something similar can be found in Waldorf schools further afield. In South America, for instance, there are Waldorf schools in the slums of huge cities, and likewise in the townships of the great metropolises of South Africa.

In Germany, too, there are other schools with socially integrative aims, as well as Waldorf special schools, either working within a facility for children with learning disabilities or as a separate school.

The outcome of such 'inclusion projects' is not yet clear, and further discussion of this is beyond the scope of the present volume.

But now let us return to the third part of the child study. How do we find adequate help or support for a child? Two things have an immediate effect on the child: the teacher with his pedagogical skills, and the curriculum subjects themselves. Before looking to other measures or interventions, we should first give due attention to these two aspects of, as it were, the natural, educational situation, and make full use of its possibilities. But before we proceed to considering this, I wish to include here something of great consequence.

The right balance between over-hasty action and procrastination

The tendency to prematurely problematize certain modes of behaviour and lack of skills is increasing today. A child must be 'diagnosed' as early as possible so that we know 'where we are'. On the one hand this is a justified aim, on the other, such an outlook considerably narrows down the picture one can gain of a child.

This is compounded by the fact that nowadays we can witness the complex repercussions of our culture and civilization. Here we need to find the right relationship to the cultural context and its effects. Let's picture a pupil who is diagnosed (early on) as having dyslexia. Naturally it's important to support this pupil immediately in the right way, with the right measures. But this is precisely where a danger awaits us: seeing this child only through the filter of his dyslexia. The same applies to all other learning difficulties. As diagnoses they tend to predetermine our view of the child, instead of us approaching him, as we should, with flexibility, creative endeavour and enquiry. The same applies to behavioural disorders or problems. They should be perceived in all acuity, but without predetermining, labelling and pigeonholing the child. This is a question, very particularly, of pedagogical creativity and openness.

Terms like dyslexia, in addition, are used very generally and therefore often imprecisely. Establishing a diagnosis of dyslexia or dyscalculia, hyperactivity or autism, tells us a great deal on the one hand, yet nothing at all on the other.

Here we have to be very alert to the question of the child's normality, despite or precisely because of specific problems. It may be that such children are much more normal than we think possible with our highly specialized knowledge. Here I would like to make a plea for a broadening of our understanding of 'normality', for more tolerance and patience in relation to certain forms of development, and trust in a person's self-healing or self-correcting capacities. Here too, the creative pedagogical ideas of the teacher directly concerned with the child can often be more effective than premature delegation to specialists – though by and large there is of course nothing to object to the latter where they are really needed. However, first and foremost, or as a first step, we should focus on the efforts of the person teaching the child day-in, day-out.

V. CONCLUDING THE CHILD STUDY

Can we help the child at all?

In this third stage of the child study, which concerns ways of helping, we need to discover firstly whether we can help at all. On the one hand one can too easily come to the conclusion that no help can be offered by the teacher or faculty, and that outside professional help is therefore needed. Equally possible is a misguided sense that one can deal with everything oneself.

While no clear parameters can be offered here, it is still vital to answer this question of whether or not help can be found within the school. Initially it must be clarified whether the child and his problem are within a normal range, and therefore are possible to remedy. (To do this, of course, we must already have sought to broaden our idea of what is normal, as described above.) An important factor here is whether or not the school has a school doctor who engages with concerns about the child in the child study. If this is so, the question can also be addressed from the medical angle.

A few examples of pedagogical support

If a decision has been made that we *can* help the pupil, we can start to draw on our pedagogical creativity and wealth of ideas. Will additional form drawings help this Class 2 pupil to activate the free part of his etheric body? Will a little verse, spoken backwards, help this child to come into himself more, since all reverse thinking/picturing draws the astral body into the etheric body? Would a very shy Class 5 pupil benefit from recitation, organized so that first the whole class speaks, then a part of the class, then just a few pupils and finally this particular child on his own? Can we help a generally weak Class 6 pupil by getting him to practice calligraphy? Would grammar relating to main and subordinate clauses and their analysis be of help to some very restless young ladies in Class 7? What part will time factors play in our measures? Can we give a child who finds it hard to remember anything a simple riddle, but ask him not to tell us the answer until tomorrow? Can we support middle school pupils who are getting too drawn out into the world by giving them biographies to read, and requiring them to give a short talk on these? Will gardening lessons have a healing effect on pupils who spend too long in front of computer screens? If a Class 1 pupil can't relate to arithmetic, Steiner recommends teaching this subject through practical activity – in other words really getting him to do something physically. Could we get him to practice sums with the aid of a large box containing a thousand white or brown beans? And if this doesn't work, even perhaps to get him to do arithmetical operations using his feet? At what point do we give a pupil with poor handwriting a series of progressively difficult form drawings, and then subsequently, in homeopathic procedure (one line a day) get him to learn a new handwriting style? What miracle can musical activity bring about as a remedy for uncontrolled will eruptions? Wouldn't it be possible in Man and Animal main lessons in Class 4 to produce a circus with the most diverse animals, so that each child identifies for a short while with a certain animal, its movements and utterances? And who would be the circus ringmaster?

Briefly, it is important to look afresh at the possibilities offered in the curriculum itself. For us teachers that is also a significant step. Anyone who engages creatively in this way, realizing something new that has not previously been tried, will very often find his efforts rewarded.

In the upper school, of course, recommendations will be adapted to the degree of maturity of each age, but here too much can be done. We have already seen the effect of getting a fairly gifted but terribly 'unavailable' and flighty Class 10 pupil to give a talk on the chameleon, including board drawings and everything necessary for this. As an adult he reported that this gave him his first experience of self-knowledge, and was decisive for his further school career. He experienced how his teachers had perceived the difficulty of his behaviour but without making moral judgements about him.

If the school has a school doctor and a eurythmy therapist, very beneficial support measures can be introduced. Here it is important that the therapist tries to present the reasons for his therapeutic measures. The whole faculty can gain in understanding from such a presentation.

Review of the support measures and their effect

It has repeatedly been reported that after a (successful) child study the child seems transformed the next day. Over time, as is also known, this phenomenon fades again. Then there are cases, too, where real and lasting change occurs towards more positive ongoing development. All these experiences lead us to the conclusion that the child study offers us a wonderful tool for understanding and helping pupils.

At the end of the child study, the chairperson summarizes the agreed measures and discusses how each will be carried out and by whom. In the review, held around eight or ten weeks later, two questions are important: Have the agreed measures been implemented? And: What effect did they have; how does the child relate to the world now? A school that creates this discipline of review has a good quality tool at its disposal. The review does not need to last more than ten minutes, and is therefore perfectly possible to fit into the schedules.

VI. HOW DO CURRICULUM SUBJECTS AFFECT CHILDREN?

Pedagogical aspects of the third part of the child study

A key idea in Waldorf education is the conscious handling of a curriculum subject to draw on its pedagogical and health-giving or even therapeutic effects. It makes a difference whether, through the subject and my manner of teaching it, I reach the child at a more pictorial level, one which addresses his whole sensibility, or instead accentuate the conceptual, more abstract side of things. Different levels of the child's nature are addressed in each case, and different inner activities are set in motion. A key suggestion of Rudolf Steiner's is to alternate between these two modes and intentionally elicit them, rather than emphasizing one at the expense of the other. In this regard he states the following:

> It is therefore necessary when teaching that we take account of whether the subject in question addresses the ether body and physical body or whether, rather, we have material that speaks to the I organization and the astral organization.[32]

The importance of the teacher's inner stance

Every teacher has had the experience that his teaching can have an enlivening, health-giving effect upon himself. Learning to overcome himself, he keeps going, and time and again tries afresh to meet the children with kindness, love and a good mood. While teaching it is absolutely legitimate to forget our daily worries for hours at a time! In fact, while teaching we seek to be the way we have actually always wished we were. At the end of the day, after teaching for six hours or so, it can seem as if we could easily go on teaching another hour. The body may be tired, but the soul is not.

Well, that may be a little exaggerated; and yet surely we all hope for this kind of fulfilment in our work. It is worth asking here how such a stance, such a relationship to our own work can affect our pupils. When this dynamic exists, something flows beautifully between teacher and class. Children look to their teacher and all his utterances and conduct as an example. He is their role model, and they experience his inner stance. Besides the content of teaching, pupils' healthy school life is based also on the sta*te of mind of the teacher himself.* Here a key principle of self-education applies: being perfect at something is not what counts, but seeking to improve. This endeavour is in fact the prime source of health for the children in a class. Steiner draws our attention to this in various passages when he characterizes the effect of the teacher's temperament on pupils.[33]

Once we have understood the importance of the teacher's inner attitude for the success of the pedagogical process, we can consider how our teaching, or more precisely the subject we are teaching, can affect our pupils. What happens in the child when he does maths? What happens in him when he writes, sings or paints? Quite apart from learning as such, all these activities also have an effect on his whole bodily and soul-spiritual state. With a more or less developed educational instinct we can have some inkling of this.

For instance, if we have practised mental arithmetic together intensively one morning, we will refrain from singing to end with for we have seen how stimulating counting and arithmetic can be, and know that singing will further stimulate the children. It would be better instead to do a form drawing or tell a story, to bring things back to a certain state of repose. If, on the other hand, we have been trying to write out a text in beautiful handwriting, we will notice how everything has grown still and quiet, perhaps even a little sleepy, and will quite naturally think of singing a song to liven things up again. We can develop an instinct for balancing things in this way, and work creatively with it. Here we already discern the effect of different subjects and activities: where one subject can enliven and awaken, another can calm and even tire the children.

The effect of teaching on the threefold human being

We must now attempt to clarify exactly how a subject affects the child's threefold nature, and exactly which aspect of it is addressed in each case. Everything that is done is taken in by the neuro-sensory system. The children *see* and *listen*, and are awake and alert in this process. But as they absorb things they also *experience* them, and this already works upon their rhythmic system. They hold their breath during an exciting experiment in physics; and when they immerse themselves in painting their breathing becomes different from when they're doing mental arithmetic together. Breathing is different again when they listen to a story or speak a poem. In other words, the breathing process in the lesson itself is reflected in that of the class.

In this realm of fluctuating experience – that acts upon breathing processes but also comes to expression through them – lies a second source of health for the child and for a whole class community.

Having reached this point in our considerations, we still need to ask how the motivation and desire of each child and the class as a whole to engage with a subject is affected by the subject itself *and* my way of teaching it. It is important to remember here that (certainly until the age of 14) the three soul faculties (thinking, feeling and will) play strongly into each other. No thought is experienced without some aspect of feeling, no activity without a felt picturing and thinking. For the teacher this means that he is on the right path if (in the lower school) he addresses the child through the powers of the middle, rhythmic system. But this in turn also means that he himself must likewise be living in and from this 'centre'. He has to address the children from the same realm that he elicits in them.

Let us return to the will forces. If our teaching has

awoken thinking and feeling, it is almost a matter of course for the child to find his way into activity. But here again the teacher's example is of special importance. Does he always do what he says? Children have a fine sense for anything that has been promised. If we do not keep our word, one can say that a 'hole' appears in the 'will body' of the class. If, for example, despite advance notice, the children's homework is not marked, or if main lesson books have not yet been looked through and returned months after the main lesson ended, or if something is threatened but not carried out, this has a negative effect on the children's will. The opposite has a healthy influence. If the teacher says, 'The day after tomorrow we will have a ball game in the hall', or, 'In one week's time I will be collecting all the books in, please make sure they're finished', and this actually happens, something healthily reliable and steady arises not just for the pupils but for the teacher himself. This has become still more important nowadays than it used to be, since experiences we can actually rely on have become rare; and this therefore has an immeasurable pedagogical dimension.

A story recounted by the theologian and priest Friedrich Rittelmeyer is illuminating here.[34] He writes:

When I look back on experiences in my youth which continued to affect me later, I discover something that ... occurred when I was eleven. One day our teacher declared, 'You must not copy from each other, but nor must you let others copy from you; this is just as bad. The supplier of stolen goods is no better than the thief.' At that age I still took teachers' words seriously; and this teacher, especially, was the only one for whom I retained a spark of veneration. It was not about being a 'goody two shoes' nor sycophancy but was my own innate scrupulousness, even a certain prizing of freedom. I had often witnessed how shaming it was when my fellow pupils were caught in the act and then had to grovel in front of the teacher with long-winded excuses. Never did I wish to be brought so low by a figure of authority! I wished to meet every teacher with freedom and assurance. But not the least understanding for such a feeling existed amongst my fellow pupils. When I refused to offer my books for others to copy, I was 'sent to Coventry': no one would speak to me. I was excluded from everything. A single pupil who wanted to go on being invited to meals at my parents' house spoke a couple of quiet words to me in a barn on one occasion, but I regarded this as especially ignominious. It was still more embarrassing when my father, who heard about what had happened, tried to intervene and make his confirmation students stop excluding me. In the end this first attempt at moral heroism on my part collapsed pitifully. I declared that I wouldn't copy from anyone, but the others could copy from me whenever they wanted. Now everything returned to normal – except that I was marked forever by a sense of moral blemish. The teacher never learned of what he had set in motion, and what had happened to the only pupil who had taken him seriously. He failed to protect me, had neither wished to nor been able to, but had left me in the lurch; indeed, had propelled me into martyrdom. In fact it was *he* who had been vanquished. And, along with all teachers and their authority, had lost my respect. Twelve years later, when I myself was to start teaching at secondary level, this memory resurfaced in me, and led to my adopting two principles in my teaching work: never demand something whose effect cannot be known and kept in control! And always maintain a vivid sense of the feelings living in the souls of pupils!

A suggestion by Rudolf Steiner is of great pedagogical scope for awakening the child's will. As we know, in the child the path to the will does not pass through the rational mind. A really central problem of education today is that the will is compelled by instruction and conceptual learning, whereas education's tasks lie in a quite different realm. We have already seen how thinking, feeling and will are interconnected: 'Feeling is growing but not yet fully developed will.'[35] And so our approach to educating the will must begin with feeling. Daily and accustomed repetitions work upon a child's soul. The same greeting each day, singing a lovely song together at the beginning of every day, speaking the morning verse together: all these are moments of recognition in which the soul can enter into warm activity. If we subtly alter something as we repeat it, we raise it from an automatic process into something that requires a small act of will, and thereby the will can be exercised and nurtured:

The more things remain an unconscious habit, the better it is for the development of feeling, while the more a child becomes aware of repeating something with engagement and commitment, because it must be done, the more you will raise this into a real impulse of will. Thus more unconscious repetition cultivates feeling while fully conscious repetition cultivates a real will impulse, for it enhances the child's power of resolve.[36]

Having briefly characterized the way in which learning can act upon thinking, feeling and will, let us now turn to the next question of how a subject itself affects the child.

What is the effect on children of the curriculum subject itself?
Image and music

Here a vast perspective opens up, and leads us to recognize the origins of a subject or discipline. We encounter polarities of eye and ear, time and space, image and tone. But at the same time we will also discover in the curriculum subject a synthesis of these opposite poles. We can ask what element of the above we are teaching out of. When do we mainly address the eye and when the ear? When are we 'in the picture', and when are we in movement, 'in flow'?

When we learn the letters with the children, when we write, draw, paint, model, and when we teach botany, we are primarily active in images and with the eyes. We are dealing with the visible realm. When we do maths or singing, when we speak poems together, when we do a concentration exercise or listen to a story, we are primarily active in a non-pictorial realm. Here we encounter a polarity that infuses all human life, within which all earthly things unfold and in which the soul lives. We can also describe this as the polarity between the *pictorial* and the *musical*.

And now we can realize that the pictorial element, above all, stands at the beginning of life: shaping, formative development leads us into life after all, and we only gradually acquire ever more form in space. This is a process beginning in the invisible realm of pre-birth reality, and coming ever more to visibility. It is also understandable, therefore, that this beginning is nourished by pre-birth forces. We enter into visibility from invisibility, from 'unborn-ness', but for a long time continue to be nurtured by these powers of the pre-birth realm. Growth creates the living picture of forms, and this is also why that fine word 'body of formative forces' was coined for the ether body. These powers from our pre-birth 'realm of origin' come to a certain conclusion of their bodily work at the age of school readiness. The powers which have formed us until then now acquire a new field of activity, becoming powers of reason, thinking and memory. All this starts to work into the child's life as a power he can make use of, and thereby intelligence reaches a certain stage of freedom.

But what about the stream of musical forces? They do not originate from before birth but work into our life from the after-death realm. These are the powers of will which slowly, as if in a long-growing crescendo, start to connect with the child. They first work in our unconscious to develop bodily functions; then, once the latter have come to a certain initial conclusion, the child's soul awakens to independence. And this moment roughly coincides with what anthroposophical terminology very accurately calls 'earth readiness', also called puberty. Now soul life attains a certain degree of freedom.

Whereas children at the start of their schooling primarily draw on pictorial forces, as the years pass these are joined by musical forces also. In the first few years of schooling, the child cannot yet respond to anything that is *too soulful*.

When telling a fairytale, for example, we can discover that the 'dramatic' element is alien to a young child and that he is only touched by more neutral realities. If no account is taken of this, and too much 'emotional' content is presented to children, something like a 'premature birth' of the soul can occur. Later, when they reach Class 6 or 7, such pupils will often display forms of behaviour in their life of feeling and will which are not sustained by adequate powers of cognition and perception. They will then lack the inner security and equilibrium enabling them to adequately manage their emotions. In the choice of class plays, for instance, we can discern whether account is being taken of the gradual unfolding of the children's psyches. The 'dramas of the soul' do come into their own in lessons, for instance in ballads, but not fully until Class 8. We are far into upper school age before a sense of tragedy is really experienced, and can invoke a response in the soul. Involvement with media products (film, TV, computer games) can muddle and confuse this gradual awakening of the soul.

The importance of stories, watercolour painting and eurythmy
Examples of the interaction of opposite poles (eye and ear, space and time, image and tone)

There are three further activities in which the polar forces interact and work together. These subjects are referred to in the Steiner curriculum. But here we should be aware that they are not just new developments since the Waldorf school began but likewise new for our whole culture. They are: storytelling as a vital pedagogical tool and core aspect of lessons, watercolour painting and eurythmy.

In storytelling we use the word, and thus a musical element, awakening however (inner) pictures in the child. When we do watercolour painting with children, and to begin with keep this in a non-figurative realm of pure colour, we are working pictorially it is true, but, through the colours, primarily engendering moods which gently touch the soul. That we are chiefly concerned with a mood is something anyone can experience who watches a class painting. Children suddenly grow quiet, without this needing to be externally imposed. Painting itself induces it in them. (Drawing, exclusively concerned with the image, is very different in this respect, and here we can often witness the children's need to talk and chatter.) In this context, eurythmy – as visible speech, as word become perceptible, as visible song (where the soul, not the voice, is the instrument) and visible music – has an astonishing effect. In eurythmy space and time extend their hand to each other, so that the audible becomes visible and the visible audible.

Aside from these three distinctive subjects, we can say that all curriculum subjects are somewhere within the described polarity. What is the relationship in other subjects? For instance, in learning to read, geography, history, botany, zoology, craft and handwork? In each case, do they work in a more pictorial and spatial, or a more musical way?

One might wonder why it is so important to answer this question. Lecture 2 of the *Foundations of Human Experience*[37] provides the key here. One can have the overpowering sense that Steiner is here establishing a new psychology in accord with contemporary needs, and in doing so focuses on two questions: What is *idea* and what is *will*?

In his account, Steiner opens the reader's eyes to the fact that all intellectual activity – such as ideation, thinking, memory and concept forming – occurs in inner images, thus involving an inner, picture-creating activity. A thought first appears in our thinking as image, and reawoken memories likewise appear in images. Thus the image or the pictorial element is the intrinsic medium in intellectual work. Steiner's comments expressly point out that this pictorial element is characterized by the quality of 'appearance' in relation to reality. In other words, I can conceive anything I like, but my idea alone does not intrinsically relate to reality or mean anything for it. Through our (inner) activity of ideation we stand before the thought picture or idea as *observers*. While we produce it ourselves, we are not it. Steiner uses the term *antipathy* to clarify this. Antipathy is a power by means of which we distance and detach ourselves from someone else or the world. From a higher standpoint it is also the power by means of which we remove ourselves from the realm of our pre-birth origin and acquire autonomy here on earth. It obscures and as it were extinguishes our awareness of our existence in the pre-birth realm. This means that the full range of our intelligent activities is oriented to pre-birth existence. At birth we then enter the spatial realm and assume bodily existence.

Everything described here receives its efficacy through the ether body. The ether body is connected with the world's ether and is at the same time the bearer of the intelligence available to us. For this reason Steiner also calls it the formative or creative body, that is, the body of formative forces, in which our habits reside. He also calls it the 'form body' and the 'learning body'. In pursuing the question of the effects of different subjects, therefore, we find that some act *primarily* on the ether body, 'teaching' it and unfolding their chief effects in it. Such subjects include form drawing, learning to read, painting and geometric drawing.

The human will as seed of the future in relation to ideation or thinking

When we enter the world, we are also born as a temporal organism. We develop in time. What role does the will play here? Human will is characterized by the fact that it can do something *now*, in this very moment. This always occurs in present time, never retrospectively. It is not the decision we made yesterday or at some point in the past that counts, but taking the action itself one has resolved upon. In other words, the will is future-oriented. It draws us onward, is the driving force in our life. It is the cause of our actions in the outer world and also within us. The actions we carry out are something *we ourselves* do. They are connected with us and compose our biography.

It is important to observe very precisely that we conduct ourselves quite differently in our thinking than in our will. Whereas we can weigh up many thinks in thought, reflect, fantasize and picture, and all this remains in the realm of thought or ideas, the will domain is quite different in this respect. Having done something, it cannot be undone again. What's done is done and there is no way back. We can imagine noble and beautiful things but at the same time have the freedom to do something far less wonderful. In thinking, with its character of appearance, we can, metaphorically speaking, stand *adjacent to the truth*. An action, by contrast, is always real, exists; and we must wait to see whether or not it is also morally sustaining as we hope. The great educational ideal of all pedagogy is to accomplish morally sustaining actions. Unlike thought life, where we can look upon ourselves, we are completely present in our actions. We realize ourselves in and through actions. For this reason we have fundamental *sympathy* towards our expressions of will, even if we subsequently feel ashamed of some things we have done. At the moment we acted, we willed this action. The will's future orientation means that it also leads us towards our death. All that was imperfect and in need of improvement in our earthly actions is stored up as seed by the will. This seed only germinates after death, and then gives us the capacity and orientation to pursue our path in the other sphere of existence, and where possible to make redress for our deeds and transform them.

Appearance and reality therefore characterize thinking on the one hand, and will on the other. In the will we are still germinal, and developing.[38] The will is fully immanent in character, which is why Steiner describes these will seeds as being 'super-real' in nature.

The organ of the will shows a strong affinity with the *astral body*. This fact is illuminating if we consider the stages of will development.[39]

If, in relation to the curriculum again, we ask which subjects *primarily* engage the astral body, we discover a different range of subjects. Through the ether body we find our way into spatial relationships, while through the astral body we find our way into the *stream of time*. Everything that works on us through language and music, works upon the will via the astral body. The musical element is will-related, living from an encounter with the world. The pictorial element by contrast is idea-related, living out of the powers that lie within me.[40]

One of Rudolf Steiner's great services was to have found in his research that the curriculum subjects do not act on pupils in a uniform or diffuse way. If a pupil draws a geometric construction, his inner corporeality is differently addressed than when he sings in the upper school choir or, in Class 8, recites a ballad with the rest of his class. The subject material always has a specific effect. It acts on the child's supersensible bodies and through these in turn again on his physical development. For this reason, if we take full account of this lawfulness, the subject material can also be used to nurture health; and it is precisely this that encompasses the task of the third part of the child study.

Thinking, picturing activities to cultivate the ether body

We have considered how the different curriculum subjects act upon the child or the pupil. Alongside the actual subject we also need to study how the *manner* of teaching, the way we teach the subject, can variously engage with the child.

Here then, taking up the quotation from Steiner at the beginning of this chapter, we will seek to find tangible answers to the question implicit in it as to how our teaching acts on the child's ether body, physical body, astral body or I organization.

Everything that calls forth picturing or thinking activity in the child, or in other words meets him as picture, primarily acts upon the physical body and the etheric body (body of formative forces). This applies to:

Figurative painting
Figurative drawings
Geometry (freehand initially then with compass and ruler)
Writing and learning to write
Form drawing
Botany
Handwork in the broadest sense

Let us now examine the more specific way these activities affect the child, firstly by considering the vital aspects of sleep and waking. When we fall asleep, something detaches itself from us. We lose our waking awareness, and all external bodily activities come to rest. The body with its subtler life functions remains in bed and our waking consciousness, along with self-awareness, vanishes. In the terminology Steiner uses in *The Foundations of Human Experience*, the spirit-soul or the soul-spirit enter the world of spirit, while the physical body remains on earth. To put it another way, the physical body and ether body remain in the bed or wherever the sleeper is, while the astral body and the I dwell in the world of spirit.

Everyone knows from their personal experience that sleep is not a static condition. Much occurs in us while we're sleeping of which we have no awareness, but whose effects we do sense. One important experience here is that of feeling refreshed, our life forces regenerated when we awaken in the morning or after a short midday nap. If we perceive more subtly we can discover that this reinvigoration does not just affect our physical and life forces but also our soul faculties or psyche. Here, primarily, we experience the effect of the ether body whose activity is intensified during the night. This activity encompasses an experience of learning, assimilation of what we absorbed and learned during the day. Steiner now describes the distinctive way in which the ether body works.[41] Its activity goes beyond what has been outlined above: one can say that it *goes on* learning at night. What was experienced during the day continues and is brought to greater completion. Even this fact is one we can partly sense. In the morning, for instance, we can wake up with answers to unresolved questions that we carried in us the evening before. Learning further, the ether body produces new insights. This indicates a rich field of enquiry and further research.

As a teacher today, if I reckon with the laws at work in the ether body then my first step will be to try to keep this knowledge alive in me, live with it, and include it in the way I shape my lessons. The nightly loss of consciousness is not just a 'hole' into which the day's experience fall, but a continued working and weaving. Next day I am not starting with a blank sheet again, but building on what has already been developed. For this reason teaching needs to offer an opportunity to bring forth these fruits again, and provide them with opportunity to unfold.

Here I'd like to mention one thing. One might assume that what has been learned in the day is taken with us into the world of spirit. But this is not the case, and these experiences are specifically *not* sustained by consciousness. In fact conscious awareness actually disrupts these learning processes, subject to etheric laws, that continue day and night!

Etherically sustained learning is quite different from something like history lessons, and we will speak later of this in detail. All that will be said here is that arithmetic cannot be grasped in the ordinary sense: it can only be *done*, and practised. Briefly, it is a habit that arises in my interaction with the world. Practising arithmetic, especially with great frequency, is – in contrast to the general view of it – a very healthy thing from the etheric perspective. One can actually sometimes regret that this wonderfully health-giving practice of arithmetic is not always valued in the way it deserves to be. The etheric body remains in bed overnight and goes on 'practising'.

History lessons have a quite different effect. If we leave aside for a moment the beautiful pictures that form part of a history main lesson, history itself depends primarily on our capacity for judgement, on the flexibility with which pupils learn to form judgements. This fact underlies the old instinct, still at work in some quarters today, not to start too early with history teaching: for judgements tax the astral body, and the latter first needs a certain maturity, a capacity for judgement. This is why Steiner also suggests studying a historical figure from *several* different perspectives.

In relation to older pupils, we can make wonderful use of this pair of opposites. Who in Class 7 or 8 will especially benefit from reading the biographies of important historical figures? Those whose capacity for judgement and inner flexibility needs strengthening! Who on the other hand will especially benefit from extra work in maths? Those in particular whose assurance in relation to the world needs supporting and consolidating, whose I-world relationship needs strengthening. A pupil whose powers of imagination are very strong but is therefore a little lacking in honesty, is helped by mathematics, not biographies. (Geometrical exercises can also be useful here.)

Taking account of the nightly after-effects of work done during the day

A second step towards awareness in modern teaching is that, as teachers, we develop a sense of trust in this ongoing, unconscious activity in the child and his etheric body. This may seem to fly in the face of current educational principles which are commonly based on conscious and cognitive learning, and early autonomy. And yet if a teacher adapts his work to mainstream requirements, and acts in line with such thinking, he will deny children full access to the creative and formative power of the etheric. Until the age of twelve, children are largely dependent on the working of the ether body as described above. Where we seek to work accordingly, our teaching will nurture health in our pupils. If we subscribe to the mistaken idea that it is good to activate the child's consciousness early on, we will later encounter and have to deal with increasing developmental hindrances. In my view the increasing phenomenon of 'difficult' children is connected with this. We can in fact sum up the task of the teacher as that of cultivating the right kind of sleeping and waking.

Cultivating the right kind of sleeping and waking

What does this mean for our hands-on work in schools? Surely that we focus more on activity and repeating activity, so that learning can become a living process rather than a merely instructional, informational type of learning. If a teacher engages with his subject matter and elaborates it so that, in a sense, he is fully fathoming it, drawing on pictures and pictorial comparisons, a great deal of his content will speak for itself and will not need to be fixed in lifeless definitions. At the same time, though, that a living pictorial quality needs to be emphasized, equally it requires a tangible connection with reality, with life, as a source of inspiration, since otherwise one might end up in the realm of fictitious or even suggestive fantasy.

The following can be an encapsulating image for this. The child has built up his body. The ship is ready. The workers who constructed the vessel are now retrained so that they can sail the boat as its crew: they become its sailors, bosun and deck hands. The helmsman and the captain, however, have not yet arrived on board.

Musical activities and those that unfold in time as
stimulus for the developing astral body

Let us now consider a few other curriculum subject.
What is the effect of

> *Zoology (Man and Animal)*
> *History*
> *Human physiology and anatomy*
> *Speech (recitation), singing and acting?*

We see that some of these subjects have more to do with
ourselves, with the human being, than do the previous
ones. Implicit in the Man and Animal lessons is the
question of how each animal relates to us. As children
discover specific qualities of animals they can experience human qualities too. The animals in a sense takes
human soul qualities to an extreme. What do I experience in the description of a lion or a mole? In history,
by contrast we become acquainted with the individual
human being as part of all humanity and can study
the outcome or repercussions of his actions. Here we
face inner questions. Was this or that historical figure
a good man or a villain? It is clear that history lessons
in the lower classes need not primarily seek objectivity
but instead living pictures of historical events. In the
upper school one can then reawaken these images and
study them with an objective eye. In the lower grades,
children's relationship to teaching content is certainly
more soulful, imbued with feeling. In the upper school
it becomes more intellectual, spiritual and therefore

objective. This is still clearer in the case of human physiology and anatomy.

As Steiner makes clear, these subjects act upon the astral body and the I organization. What does this mean? Let's picture a lower-school child. His soul responds to and resonates with life (thus also school life), with the thoughts and feelings of others around him. Only gradually does he emerge from the mood of his surroundings into autonomous work and learning. He first has to awaken, if you like, before he can independently engage with a subject. As we can discover when teaching, there are huge differences between children. But in the lower school we can start from the assumption that the psyche (astral body) and I organization *within* the child do not yet have the maturity to be autonomous. This is one reason in fact why teaching of subjects is related to particular ages and stages of development. Additionally, says Steiner, teaching of *these* subjects is something 'that a person takes with him from the physical and ether body into the spiritual world when he falls asleep'. In other words, these particular subjects, unlike the others mentioned above which nurture the life of thinking, are *not* 'learned further' by the ether body during sleep. In fact, during sleep there is a 'tendency' for their effect on the soul-spiritual organism to be such that what has been learned is forgotten. This content, as Steiner describes it, becomes 'less perfect' and 'pale'.[42]

Something we may already have vaguely sensed while teaching becomes clearly apparent here as a starkly contrasting effect on children. We can now understand that we should try with these curriculum subjects to establish a relationship with the etheric body. We can do so if we draw on pictorial description, on images, thus teaching in graphic and vivid ways. This effect on the ether body can best be achieved by giving as vivid and tangible a description as we can of, say, an historical occurrence, a plant or the human skeleton.

Having done so, the next step is to add a kind of characterizing postscript, now no longer in pictorial mode. We are no longer as it were within the phenomenon but are describing it from without. This approach addresses the *psyche*, whereas the other speaks to the *ether body*. Then we round off the theme. Steiner says of this procedure that the subject matter handled in this way can fix itself like a *photograph* in the ether body during the following night. We pick up on this the next day when – in an age-appropriate way – we review and evaluate with the children what we did the day before. Thus we establish here a connection between the child's physical-etheric and soul-spiritual nature.

Young teachers may sometimes feel that this way of working is rather artificial and appears unspontaneous. But if one just tries these suggestions as an experiment, one finds they do actually work, and that this makes teaching considerably easier. Repeatedly using this methodology in fact enables it to develop into a kind of 'instinct' for the right approach when teaching.[43] Certainly, for instance, it can free the teacher from the trap of approaching history just as 'story-time'.

The special nature of geography, arithmetic and geometry

Geography
Steiner says that geography has the following effect:

> Seen in spatial terms, when we do geography with the child, this always makes the astral body stand up as it were. It actually becomes denser and stronger below. We drive what is spatial in nature downward towards the ground, thus making the soul and spirit denser.

At a deeper level, therefore, geography lessons – in other words, enquiry into the spatial realm of earth – also act as an aid to incarnation. The child's soul and spirit connects with spatial, earthly conditions, and, one can say, arrives on earth. Steiner further explains that geography awakens in children a sense of fellow feeling with all other human beings. He says that a child will have a more loving relationship to others if he has been taught geography in a 'judicious' way. He assigns this to age 11 and over.[44]

When geography is taught in a 'judicious' way, as we learn from Rudolf Steiner's own research, it consolidates the soul and spirit, rooting and anchoring it. Interest in the spatial world, additionally, has an effect on our soul capacities as earthly human beings; here too we find a gesture of connection, but now with other human beings, and this can shed light on the statement that geography teaching can have a moral outcome.

Steiner unmistakably characterizes the great import of this subject when he says: '... and suppression of geography means nothing other than an aversion to love of one's fellow human beings, which has increasingly been suppressed in our age.'

But geography's greatest importance of all can be found in relation to the subtle yet highly significant developmental step which occurs in children approaching the age of ten. Learning at this age to distinguish himself more from the surrounding world we can see how all the aspects of geography outlined briefly above can accompany the child. Geography is, in a sense, the key midwife in this birth process, which usually occurs quietly and out of sight. Steiner once referred to this stage as a 'crossing of the Rubicon', and since then this has been a phrase much used in the Waldorf movement. But what does it actually mean? It means crossing a border and entering new territory, and doing so in a way that makes return impossible. The soul has taken a defining step, resolving to enter into the world in all its beauty but also all its risks. When is it able to risk this step? Only when it has achieved independence in a part of the astral body that serves bodily processes, and released another part so as to engage with the world. Downward anchoring and consolidation, and partial upward emancipation. (Full emancipation then occurs at puberty, which we know signifies more than just sexual maturation.) We can also say that the child leaves the golden age of childhood, departs from paradise; and this process is wonderfully reflected in local geography lessons at this age. What does this imply for the child study?

As teachers, have we learned to perceive in our pupils the subtle process which Steiner calls 'crossing the Rubicon'? Do we notice the child who unexpectedly withdraws? Do we see what is going on in the child who suddenly seeks more closeness and reassurance and, years after giving up this habit, wants to come and sit on the teacher's lap again? Do we notice the boys who don't quite know how to conduct themselves, and do we attend to sudden, unexpected anxieties? And then also, sometimes very surprisingly, three or four parents may be knocking on the door and feeling unsure about the school. A previously established order suddenly enters choppy waters.

But now comes a local geography main lesson, and the teacher is pleased because he knows that it will enable him to lead the children out into part of their surrounding world. That, if you like, is the ordinary course of things. Its *added value*, however, comes *if the teacher knows* that this subject offers a kind of soul comfort to the child at his present stage of development. We could put it like this: You may now enter the world; this subject offers you assurance and clear direction.

Seeing some of our pupils anxiously hold back from this threshold, in geography we really do have a loving midwife who will give us great help if we know this and can teach the subject with this in mind.

History
In teaching history we can sense how this speaks to another part of the soul. We can say that history occu-

pies a 'higher realm' compared with geography. It is less concerned with spatial conditions but with the temporal course of particular events, with human biographies and human actions. The subject acts on the soul in a structuring and 'sculpting' way, prompting children to form stronger feeling judgements – for instance, this person was a hero, while the other was somewhat cowardly; one person acted wisely while another was reckless; and so on. So here we are more concerned with the psychological and emotional realm, and we can observe that geography addresses the *feeling will* while history evokes our *feeling thinking*.

Arithmetic and geometry

I will preface this by noting that whereas we should very carefully consider the right moment for introducing other subjects (learning to read, history, geology, part-singing, physics, chemistry etc.), there are no such concerns in relation to arithmetic: we do it the whole time, from Class 1 to Class 12. This can tell us that it exists as a universal human capacity and potential from the moment we are able to think and enter into a relationship with the world. Measure and number inform and order the world. We can see that arithmetic begins as soon as the child starts to be aware of different categories of things, and these beginnings soon develop into a higher art of mathematics that no longer requires the tangible world.

In this context, the following statement by Steiner on arithmetic can raise a heartfelt cheer. He first refers to the diverse effects of different subjects as we have been considering them, in particular distinguishing how they tend more to nurture the etheric and physical body on the one hand, or the astral body and soul on the other, and what happens in the night to these experiences. Then he turns to arithmetic and geometry: 'Arithmetic and geometry address both these realms, that is the remarkable thing.' In other words, they affect both the etheric-physical and the soul-spirit. And he continues: 'And for this reason one can say that as regards teaching and education, both arithmetic and geometry are a kind of chameleon: by their very nature they adapt themselves to the whole human being.'[45]

These sentences contain some important secrets. All the other subjects so far discussed are potentially one-sided in their effect, and this should be considered when teaching them. (For instance, Rudolf Steiner recommends that the child should only learn to read when he himself 'wishes to'. And he considers it important not to present intellectualized subjects too early, nor prematurely cultivate a faculty of judgement etc.) When we come to arithmetic we find the opposite: the subject itself adapts to the child in his whole nature. In other words: there is no lower age limit for it.

This tells us why children can always count and do arithmetic (though naturally in age-appropriate ways) and why, as we have heard, arithmetic contains powers that can nurture children's health and in fact address the 'whole human being'. This means that the activity of arithmetic itself has a deep affinity with the human being. And there is a certain tragedy in the fact that this is misunderstood in the contemporary world by such a one-sided emphasis, and thus pressure upon it. Almost all curriculum subjects today are 'mathematized' so that aversions to this wonderful activity develop and lead to the very opposite of what arithmetic and mathematics can give us. Mathematics deserves to be redeemed from misappropriation so that children can take real pleasure in the subject itself and, as consequence of this, also in its applications in life.

As already suggested, soul activities (such as the capacity for judgement) can only be called on to a limited degree in the lower school. The same is true in the upper school of I activity (such as resolving to do what one considers right). In both cases the potential for these faculties has not yet been liberated. All teaching works towards this emancipation. The reticence Steiner urges regarding premature development of these capacities can be pictured in the following metaphor: you can't play on a violin that is still being made; if you do string it before it's finished and start bowing, you won't get much of a tone out of the instrument.

Steiner does not enter into long-winded explanations when he describes these things. He merely says that, if summoned too early, without due understanding, the astral and I organization act only sluggishly by comparison with the ether body's dynamic affinity with learning. The ether body however goes on doing arithmetic, and goes on drawing forms during the night, perfecting the skills that were practised during the day, thus giving the child a feeling of delight and in turn kindling the will. In other words, if we do arithmetic in such a way that only feeling understands what we are doing, continuing and repeating this, we not only learn arithmetic but also strengthen the body of formative forces and the soul body – the latter specifically by leaving it in peace.

We should dwell on this a little, for it represents a principle intrinsic to Waldorf pedagogy. Arithmetic today is ensnared in the forces of egotism; and we can discern this, for instance, in the way politics is now really only driven by business and finance, in the fact that the plus sign (+) on a pocket calculator is four times larger than the signs for division, subtraction or multiplication, and in the way world events are surveyed largely or primarily in financial terms. But if we draw on *this* mindset, we render the healing effect of arithmetic on the 'whole human being' null and void! Then mathematics serves only an aim divorced from human concerns.

If we try to grasp this, it becomes apparent how arithmetic does actually work upon the physical-etheric and the soul-spirit.

Steiner, as we know, recommended that arithmetic should *not be developed from addition* but from division, thus proceeding from a unity. Let us consider this more carefully. Language itself here offers us some guidance in seeing unity as the first and highest principle. We speak of the 'first among equals', of the first prize; and of people who are the 'first' in their field. The One, the unity, the whole is the background to such sayings, and is the creative principle from which the world unfolds. We can also call it God. Everything arose from this 'first principle'. Addition, by contrast, gives a picture of the gathering together of what has previously been divided up, and thus detached from the whole; and as such has a moral aspect that addresses soul and spirit. This alone would be a good reason for not beginning arithmetic teaching with it. A further reason, grounded in human nature, is that addition is not an activity corresponding to the ether body's self-dividing activity. Adding is alien to the ether body whereas it recognizes itself in all dividing and inwardly structuring activities. Once this dividing activity has been anchored in arithmetic lessons, additive counting will no longer do any harm. Adding, says Steiner, 'is an activity that only has significance here in physical space, whereas subdivisions of a unity are such that they continue to reverberate in the etheric body, even when we are not aware of this'.[46]

Finally, I'd like to say this. Precisely because it depends so much on the interactions between our 'upper' and 'lower' systems, what is true of all teaching applies to arithmetic and geometry to a still greater degree: it must be engaging, must awaken interest and draw on life. If we manage to do this, we have opened up a rejuvenating source of physical and soul health.

Craft, handwork, gymnastics and gardening
Our gaze turns to a quite different realm when we consider these subjects, in which, naturally, physical activity is the prime experience. What do such activities signify for pupils?

So far, in our efforts to find perspectives in education corresponding to our deeper human nature, we have considered the polarities of pre-birth and after-death, idea and will, and image and tone. Now we must turn to another such polarity.

The polarity between the human being's physical and spiritual nature

The spirit is at the other end of the scale from physical corporeality. At an initial, quite mundane level we can experience how these two poles are connected. No doubt we have all had the experience of making great efforts in the run-up to an exam, perhaps studying and revising all day. After a day like that you can feel more tired than after physical exertion. This is further intensified if you work through the night. The body has to pay the price of the intellect's efforts. The opposite is equally common: physical work can regenerate the mind and refresh it. Thus physical activity and mental exertion have a mutual interaction, and it can be very useful to learn how to manage this swinging back and forth between the two. How does this reciprocity work in education?

The teacher should be aware that the human being's movement will is a mystery! While science has decoded almost all the secrets of genetics, something as ordinary as the following still remains hidden. How does it come about that the moment I think of taking a step or lifting a cup to my mouth, this actually occurs? How can we explain this mystery of movement? Or to put it another way, how is an intention I form actually realized? Science fails to ask these questions since – in Steiner's view

– it mistakenly assumes that our nerves issue the command, say, to extend an arm, and then pass it on to be carried out. Steiner asserts, by contrast, that nerves can only perceive movements, not initiate them. The transition from idea to action, he says, is a spiritual process without a physical correlation at the key point of transition between the intention formed in our mind or reason and its realization in the body. There is a 'gap' here. (If we look at finger skills used in handwriting or piano playing, and consider that all these movements are willed by an I, we can discern the open secret of will and movement occurring before our eyes.) Only very gradually is modern science unveiling this mystery, and starting to confirm what Steiner stated.

In this context we can now also understand Steiner's statement that 'you are continually splashing about in spirit, continually involved with spirit, when you move your limbs to work – whether the work is useful or not'. We surely will be on the right track if we view the spirit here as a supersensible *activity* rather than a *state* of consciousness. Yet this is a remarkable kind of spirituality. Just as we bear a soul and spirit within us, and are partly aware of it – and can therefore work on and with it – so a soul and spirit also exists in the world outside us. Here we encounter a quite new polarity, that of inner and outer, point and periphery. Thus we can entertain the following thought and to some degree experience its reality:

When we work physically, our soul and spirit participates in this only insofar as we direct our actions and motions through thoughts, orienting ourselves in thought. But external soul and spirit is fully involved. We continually work into the spirit of the world, continually connecting with it, by working physically. Bodily work is spiritual, spiritual work is bodily, undertaken in and upon the human being ... The spirit washes around us as we work physically, while matter is vitalized in us as we work spiritually.[47]

Here we have insights that go in two directions: so-called physical work is spiritual in nature while so-called spiritual work (including learning in the stricter sense) works upon our physical corporeality.

Eurythmy as an activity that harmonizes body and spirit

What is described here also sheds light on eurythmy, this remarkable offspring of Rudolf Steiner's insights. Others are better qualified to speak of this domain, but in the context with which we are here concerned Steiner himself characterizes how eurythmy relates spirit and body. Following on from his words above, he shows that all organs participating in eurythmy are imbued with spirit. Through eurythmy's intentional movements, the spirit releases itself from our organs and streams upwards. This acts like 'a redemption of the spirit ... The spirit, with which our limbs are brimming, is released. That is what actually happens.'

He then goes on to describe how the 'liberated' spirit is waiting to be employed, to manifest in the human being. And then comes the powerful thought that this is accomplished by a subsequent moment of rest. In eurythmy, therefore, we accomplish a process which is truly a microcosm of the macrocosmic law of movement – which is spirit – and of the macrocosmic law of repose, which is matter.[48]

Instead of western education being wholly revolutionized by this insight, it carried on along the old tracks, continuing to further separate the realms of spirit and matter from each other. We can see this in the one-sided nature of sports and athletics which have become an end in themselves. (Steiner commented critically that 'sport is practical Darwinism'.[49]) We can see this also in the learning culture at mainstream schools with its increasing regard for 'achievement' or grades as an end in themselves, without much concern for the pupil's relationship to or assimilation of the content he has learned. Mental (spiritual) work, accomplished by sitting still has come ever further adrift from movement (sport, outdoor activities).

Clearly the middle realm is lacking here. Conceptual thinking is practised, the head burdened, and this one-sided exertion is then compensated for by sport. The centre is not addressed. Thus feelings remain body-bound (desires, drives) or cling to thinking (fantasies, emotions). In psychological terms, thinking and will are cultivated while feeling as an autonomous faculty is only feebly developed. In physiological terms this means that the neuro-sensory system and the system of metabolism and limbs become excessive in scope while the rhythmic system atrophies. We can say that spirit and body are cultivated while the soul or psyche is ignored.

In consequence of this distorted picture, the mission of Steiner's art of education can become apparent to us. To fully clarify what I mean, I will quote once again from Friedrich Rittelmeyer's autobiography.[50] In my view, his perceptions are still very relevant:

> Unfortunately I have to say of my secondary education that none of our teachers succeeded, except at very rare and fleeting moments, in awakening our heartfelt engagement with their subject. Everything felt like hard labour from start to finish. As far as I am aware, none of my fellow pupils ever, even in misguided moments, thought that one could be interested in what one had to learn. Anything of interest happened after school, when four o'clock finally came. Arriving at university and meeting pupils from other schools, I was filled – already at that age – with fury when I saw what crimes had been committed upon our young souls. The damage done by refusing young hearts the life elixir of enthusiasm can never be remedied again in the rest of one's life.

Against what Rittelmeyer experienced in his youth, we can set a new kind of education whose mission is to harmoniously connect these two realms with each other. In our pedagogy we fill physical exertion with *meaning and purpose*, and spiritual, intellectual learning processes with *interest*. To put it another way, we could also describe this process as one of harmonizing light and warmth. Once we understand this, we can also see what Steiner means when he urges that lessons should echo on in the soul, not only allowing what has been learned to be retained, but the *act of learning* itself to become part of the child's soul content:

> What children do in learning to read condenses into the capacity to read; what they do in learning arithmetic condenses into the capacity for arithmetic. But now consider things related more to feeling and memory: here children learn, really, an endless amount solely in order to forget it again, simply so that they don't have to think about it any more in their lives. An education of the future will be distinguished very particularly by the fact that everything the child learns will live on in him for the rest of his life.[51]

Here we can apply Goethe's (often misunderstood) phrase: 'Consider what you do, but still more how you do it.'

Let me give two examples. In our school, when I was young, we had a highly esteemed teacher of German. Everything he did with us felt inspired and creatively original, whether he was teaching us grammar or literature. His name was Matthieu Laffrée. One day he told us that we would be reading together the little book by Gottfried August Buerger entitled 'Marvellous

Travels on Water and Land: Campaigns and Comical Adventures of Baron Muenchhausen'. We not only thought this text rather inane but, in Class 11, felt we had more important things to do with our time. He sensed our unwillingness, smiled at our presumption, and suggested that we should nevertheless read at least a few passages from the book at least. OK, so we read this seemingly inane story about the baron who pulls himself and his horse out of a swamp by his own hair. But the question remained for us: why were we reading this nonsense as an example of German Romanticism? Over twenty years later, the key image in this story suddenly dawned on me as a metaphor for someone always capable of picking himself up off the ground, changing and reshaping himself. This sudden insight was accompanied by a step in self-knowledge: a warm sense of gratitude rose in me, for what I had learned, that had carried on working within me. It was as if my teacher was giving me a friendly wave from the other side.

Our teacher of chemistry and biology was outstanding in his attention to phenomena, and one of the first to introduce Goetheanism into the sciences by rigorously pursuing his own observations and observational practice. His written works are still full of a sense of germinal potency. His name was Frits Julius. Though we were his students, we were not yet fully aware how brilliant he was, though his chemistry lessons, when he stood at the experiment table, struck us as a form of religious rite for the natural world. In my report for Class 11 he assessed my efforts and the skills I had acquired in biology and chemistry; but he ended with the following remarkable sentence: 'How do things stand with your love of sense perception?' Reading this, I thought to myself, well, there's nothing wrong there. Only much, much later I realized that this specifically was a weakness in my character; and the sentence has accompanied me throughout my life as a quiet yet powerful admonition.

Let us now return to the third stage of the child study and gather the threads of all that we have so far considered in the question: How do we help the child or pupil who stands before us? We have seen that it can be necessary to find special therapeutic measures. But having considered the diverse qualities of curriculum subjects, we have also seen how lessons *themselves* can affect the child most beneficially. To put it very succinctly, teaching itself can have healing effects.

Four polarities in the reciprocal effects of the supersensible bodies

There is a further means of making lessons into a healing process, though this may not arise in a child study. A lone teacher can pursue it by adopting a different stance towards his teaching. It is a path that has something in common with what has been outlined above but takes differentiation in teaching a step or two further. Here I will first describe it briefly, and later discuss its specific applications in more detail.

Alongside the great foundations of his anthropology

(in *Foundations of Human Experience*) Rudolf Steiner also gave teachers four further perspectives, introduced at various points, with whose help we can come closer to understanding the growing child. They involve the following four polarities:

Large-headed – small-headed
Rich in imagination – poor in imagination
Cosmic – earthly
The I is too strongly – too weakly present
in the body.

These four encapsulate the secret of the interrelation between the four bodies: the physical body, where the polarity is apparent as a contrast between a relatively large or relatively small head; the level of the life body (ether body) as contrast between the qualities of a rich or poor imagination; the sphere of the astral body (soul) as field of tension between the two extremes of cosmic and earthly; and finally the domain of the I in its immersion in, or lack of engagement with, the physical body.

'Large-headed' – 'small-headed' children

The contrast between large-headed and small-headed children can be found in the faculty meeting transcripts (CW 300b, meeting of 6 February 1923) and has already led to a great deal of misunderstanding. Are we talking about an absolute or even measured size? Does this refer to the relationship between the head and the rest of the body? Examination of the precise context of the discussion can – as so often – help us here. (Again, though, let us be clear that we are decidedly not speaking of some kind of direct psycho-physical coupling or even of an antiquated characterology as developed in the 19th and early 20th centuries. Steiner's efforts are directed here to perceiving the *true condition* of a child by observing his outward form and modes of expression. He was convinced that the child is still mobile and flexible enough to allow the spirit to manifest in the body.) The listed polarities are intended *as aids to better observation*.

The faculty meeting begins with Steiner saying that he wishes to discuss child health issues relevant to teaching and to first offer some founding principles. He then explains the threefold nature of the human organism: neuro-sensory system, rhythmic system and the system of limbs and metabolism. Then he asks the teachers to say, from their observations, whether they think one of the systems is predominant in pupils and, if this is the case, to take healthcare measures of either a medical or dietary nature. Steiner points out that children's utterances and forms of expression can enable us to perceive which system dominates. Then he changes perspective and explains how one can also discover which system is predominant by observing the child's outward form; and follows this by contrasting large-headed with smaller-headed children.

Steiner characterizes the large-headed children as 'phlegmatic' or 'sanguine', saying they tend to have fleeting or short attention. One should help them, he says, to stimulate the formative forces which will enable them to be more attentive to the outer world. As health measure he suggests a diet rich in salty foods: 'With a head that is especially large, therefore, we find what I have now described as deficiencies arising from fleeting attention and excessive phlegm.' By contrast, in children whose head is relatively small we can detect a weakness of the metabolic system. The latter does still carry out its task for the whole organism, but no more than that. One sees, says Steiner, that these children often 'brood on things', but on the other hand are much irritated by outward impressions and react too strongly to them. Here it would be helpful, he goes on, to introduce a sweeter diet.

In addition one should consider the way a child thinks, the whole way he *acquires* ideas. Here, therefore, we pass on from an external to an inner observation. In this way Steiner gradually characterizes what he meant when he spoke of 'large-headed' and then 'small-headed' (a distinguishing characteristic that is no longer mentioned in the rest of the text).

When a child shows little inclination for discernment in thinking, lumping everything together in his mind and unable to make clear distinctions, the neuro-sensory system is not working properly. The effort one has to make with the child to get him to be more analytic is at the same time the symptom of something wrong in the neuro-sensory system, and one then needs to approach the problem in the way I have described.

Where a child has too little capacity for synthetic or constructive thinking and is therefore unable to picture things, is a kind of little barbarian when it comes to art, as is very often the case in children today, then this is a symptom that the system of limbs and metabolism is not in order, and then we need to seek help from the other side of things, giving him more sugar. This is generally very important, also in regard to health and therapy, that we discern whether the child is lacking either in a capacity for analytic or synthetic thinking.

There is something else as well. Imagine you have a child who is clearly lacking in this ability to think analytically: this can also be a sign that the child is diverting his astral body and I too much away from his neuro-sensory system; and then one has to ensure somehow or other that the child is washed with cool water in the morning.

In the opposite case, where a child is inartistic, and lacks the element of synthetic, constructive thinking, so that he does not warmly engage with what you're trying to teach him, the astral body is reluctant to properly engage in the system of limbs and metabolism; and then one has to try to support the child by keeping the stomach organs really warm at some appropriate time.[52]

This section is of radical importance, and gives us insight into the way soul and body are connected or, to put it another way, how the soul can be influenced and affected by the body. This is fundamental to the whole approach to child health in a school. Steiner continues:

> Such things should not be underestimated, for they are extremely important. If you have a child who has no inclination to paint or do music, it really is not some kind of materialistic aberration to advise parents to give him a warm stomach compress two or three times a week at bedtime, keeping it warm through the night.
>
> You see, people are too dismissive of material measures and over-estimate the value of abstract, intellectual approaches. But we should try to correct this erroneous contemporary view by realizing that the divine powers employ their spirit for the earth so as to materially achieve everything they do. The divine, spiritual powers make things warm in summer and cold in winter. It would be mistaken for them to seek to achieve with us by intellectual or moral instruction what they accomplish with humankind by enabling us to sweat in summer and shiver in winter. Therefore you should not underestimate the effect of material interventions for children. We should always consider such things.[53]

In the subsequent sections Steiner also refers to the teacher as a 'prophylactic physician'. Today, sadly, our school practice is far removed from such measures. But when one resorts to them it should always be a self-evident procedure that everything undertaken in relation to the pupil's physical body, whether as external application, or medicine and diet, happens by recommendation and with the supervision of a school doctor, and with the parents' full agreement.

We can see from the way this theme was dealt with in the meeting with Rudolf Steiner, and the responses from teachers, that this outlook never got very far. When the school doctor refers to it again later, saying he cannot concur, Steiner replies that he, the physician, does not yet have the right foundations for perceiving these things. He dwells a little on the nature of a weak metabolism; and having described this asks how a child appears in the class if his metabolism is strong and fully developed. It seems that these are children with big hands, and strongly formed arms and legs, thus demonstrating that they have directed more energy into forming their body than into developing their head. What, therefore, is the nature of these children's attention and thinking?

Aren't these the children who tend to be 'bright' in their head, who easily grasp things and possess analytic thinking from an early age? Have we here characterized a 'small-headed' disposition; or is the small-headed disposition related to a weak metabolism? And what does a child look like in whom the rhythmic system is fully enough developed so that both poles can unite in equilibrium?

These considerations arise in the context of Rudolf Steiner's description of how intelligence develops through pre-birth powers, the latter using the child's head as gateway through which they continue to form the body until the age of rising seven. At the change of teeth these body-forming forces come to a conclusion, withdraw from the body and come to expression in the ability to paint, draw and model. They are 'sculptural forces', and now encounter the pre-birth powers that continue working in the child as powers of intelligence. This 'collision' comes to physical expression in the change of teeth, and inwardly in the appearance of a free intelligence not solely tied to bodily processes. Intelligence works down from above, in contrast to the modelling forces that work up from below. This process now also determines the extent to which the head allows cosmic powers through or retains them. What does this mean for the child as he develops? Rudolf Steiner says:

> If the child later becomes a sculptor, a draftsman or architect – but I mean a real architect who works out of forms – this occurs because such a person has the predisposition to retain in his organism somewhat more of the powers that stream down into his organism, to retain more of these in his head, so that these childhood powers still continue to stream down later. But if they are not held back, if everything passes into the soul realm at the change of teeth, we have children without any predisposition for drawing, sculpting or architecture, who can never become sculptors.
>
> That is the mystery: these powers are connected with what we underwent between death and our latest birth.

Does this mystery also contain the answer to the question of large or smaller heads? The next question that arises is this: if pre-birth powers are not held back or retained in the head, does this also mean no disposition will arise for musical gifts in the child – which appear when the astral forces work upon the child, again through the head, and are then suppressed at the next major developmental watershed of puberty? These questions can preoccupy one for a long time. At all events, this perspective on things can, despite being only briefly outlined, give us a sense of what a person prepares for his bodily development in pre-birth existence. It is also appropriate to ask here whether there is a connection between the processes involved in relatively larger or smaller head development, as a polarity that comes to expression in the physical realm (a matter discussed in lecture 2 of *Balance in Teaching*, Stuttgart, 16 September 1920, CW 302a).

Children with a strong or weak imagination

To understand the polarity of children with either a weaker or stronger imagination we need to study the relevant text passage very carefully, even though it is only short. First let me say something about the time and place where these comments were made. Steiner made them to the teachers of the first Waldorf school in the summer of 1921 – thus the end of the year – and was reviewing the first two years of the school's work and also looking forward to the forthcoming school year. In the next year the school was to establish a Class 10. In GA 302, entitled *Waldorf Education for Adolescence*

– formerly called the 'supplementary course' – we find wonderful passages on the psychology of puberty. Here therefore we need to be aware that this 'perspective' on imagination was given in a specific context and situation. From this one might conclude that the question of children being either weak or strong in imagination is one that concerns the upper school more than the lower school. This is confirmed by Steiner's remark on the imaginative faculty between the ages of 12 and 15 in lecture 14 of *The Foundations of Human Experience*, which relates to pupils in Class 9 and 10. The way in which Steiner is using the term 'imagination' can potentially cause confusion. Nowadays we use the word in its narrower sense to describe the capacity to create something original by thinking or working imaginatively. At the beginning of Steiner's comments he does refer to this common understanding when he says that being strongly imaginative does not mean that children will immediately become poets. What he means, rather, is a capacity to retain the mental pictures which arise after experiencing or hearing something. This explains the close connection of this capacity with memory. (Here we should recall that the supplementary course begins with Steiner stating that many things have developed very well, but that things learned have not been sufficiently retained; and then he goes on to speak of the power of memory and retention.)

We can notice whether a child tends more towards a strong or weak imagination, says Steiner,

less in the activation of imagination itself than in

the development of memory. Memory has a strong affinity with imagination. You see, we have children – and we must observe this – who quickly forget the images of what they have heard or experienced. Their memory pictures easily fade. Other children retain such images, which acquire more or less an independent power in them, continually surfacing unbidden. It is good to notice that these two different types exist. Naturally there are all possible transitions between them.[54]

Here's an example: In Class 8 we read a story to the pupils and then ask them to recount or write down what they 'saw' inwardly while listening. If we compare the outcome, we can easily see what is meant here. Or the following observation can illustrate it: various different people recount an episode from their life. We will notice that in some accounts we can really 'see' almost everything that is related – whole tableaus or panoramas appear before us. But there will also be accounts with very little to be 'seen', in which things just 'happen'.

One can also have the following striking experience. Reading a book awakens inner images in us. When we later see a film of the book, we can find that our own images clash with those of the film; and here we can witness our own imaginative activity colliding with 'alien' images.

In his account, Steiner goes on to describe children who are really 'plagued' by their mental pictures, which surface even when not summoned. This means that there are inner images which enter into no direct relationship with what one is doing or thinking at any moment; or also that certain actions may be inevitably connected with certain inner pictures or thoughts. A pupil once told me that whenever he had to wash and dry the dishes and cutlery at home, he always saw images of ships which he had to direct to their harbour moorings. He said these images arose involuntarily as soon as he started washing dishes. Here someone is being 'plagued' by his strong imagination or, in Steiner's words, the pupil is the 'prisoner' of his own thoughts.

A remedy is to give such pupils more painting and handwriting, or in other words let them carry out more movements, whereas children who have forgotten their inner images ought rather to practise observation – which can usefully also include the observation of words and sentences while reading. We can do more here too in music lessons by alternating between singing and listening to singing. This enables the 'learning body' to connect with the soul body, the etheric with the astral. Producing tones is different from listening to them. The latter involves the soul element. The following shows the degree of differentiation which Steiner envisages in the way teachers handle lessons: account should be taken of those strong or weak in imagination, he says, in recitation and eurythmy. Children with a weak memory can be helped by getting them to speak poems with more and more consonantal quality. Those who tend to be plagued by their thoughts and inner images should practise poems with a stronger vowel quality, in eurythmy too. In addition, those with a weak imagination should mainly do eurythmy while standing still, that is, 'chiefly with their arms'. Those with a strong imagination, on the other hand, should use their whole body, in 'running, walking and stepping'.

We should always remember that such characterizations are relative conditions. And yet we all, surely, know of pupils whose memory is cause for concern. Instead of some kind of 'memory training' in the usual sense, we can try to gently nurture the foundations that lead to a capacity for inner picturing. Ought we not to try this at least, however modest in scope? Later we will see some of the means available for this in an artistic approach to teaching.

At the end of his presentation, Steiner returns to the subject of learning by heart, emphasizing that children should always have some feeling involvement in what they learn. An important pedagogical rule of thumb here is this: whatever tends towards the dramatic or tragic works on the metabolism, while all that leads us more into beauty and light-heartedness works upon the neuro-sensory system.

The earthly-cosmic polarity

It is again important to recall the context in which Steiner elaborates this theme. Two things should be considered in this context. In order to rightly understand what is involved we first need to imbue ourselves with the sense that the human head actually has little to do with inheritance since it is a reflection or image of the cosmos, and thus an expression of it. The fact that our head may resemble those of family members is due simply to the head being a part of the whole, and therefore affected by it. Our limbs and trunk are more truly inherited. Secondly, we must take on board an aspect of methodology. If we wish to gain greater understanding of the human being we ought not to make do with the polarity of spirit and soul on the one hand, and the physical and etheric on the other. Rather, we should trace how the spirit and soul work right through into the physical body for otherwise, as Steiner says, 'we have nothing real'. The physical body must be seen as an expression of the whole human being. In this way, an abstract grasp of the human being can move on into a fluid, dynamic and artistic grasp. (The contrast between head, limbs and trunk is presented at length in lecture 4 of *Balance in Teaching*, CW 302a.) Steiner does not see these contrasts as mutually exclusive; and he elaborates this in very drastic words in the preface to his remarks on children's cosmic or earthly orientation:

> If one stands on the foundation of spiritual science or anthroposophy, it really doesn't matter whether one is a 'materialist' or 'spiritualist'. You see, if you really pursue things to their conclusion, everything is transformed into spirit.

Thus, if we think world phenomena all the way through consistently, the (one-sided) materialist, says Steiner, turns out to be 'weak-minded' and the (one-sided) spiritualist 'barmy'. In the further lectures much is concealed which we might call 'composition secrets'. It seems to me that the whole introduction, here briefly described, is in fact an account of how cosmic and earthly are interfused in the life of humanity; and that these descriptions aim to make us aware of the inter-relationship of 'above' and 'below' before we start to observe how these work in the child.

While, in the polarity between weak and strong imagination discussed earlier, there is no point of ref-erence in the child's physical body, in the case of the cosmic-earthly contrast we do have this: the 'sculptural shaping of the head' in the case of the 'cosmic' child, and the 'sculptural modelling of the rest of the human form, that is, of the limbs' in the case of the 'earthly child'. How do we perceive such a thing? Here we have an opportunity to practise artistic perception of something in dynamic movement. How can we tell if a child's being stresses the sculptural shaping of his arms and legs? Surely this is a gesture of his form and figure? Can't we see a certain emphasis on sculptural expres-sion of the arm which appears (or does not appear) as manifestation of the self? Take a look at a twelve-year-old or sixteen-year-old and try to discern this expres-sive power of the hands or legs. Can we gain an inkling here of what Steiner means? Is there a certain emphasis placed on beauty of expression in the limbs? Let us try the same with the head. How characteristic is it? We have no doubt sometimes seen people whose head and face, relative to their age, seems somewhat unformed, and may even appear like a 'baby-face'. But we also know children to whose head our gaze is invariably drawn, and seems to have so much to tell us because the whole child comes to expression there. The following passage is key as we approach this mode of observation:

> Now, it is very important to complement everything else we have considered in relation to fathoming the child's being by trying to discern whether cosmic organization predominates – apparent in a modelling and shaping of the whole head – or whether earthly organization is particularly salient. The latter will be apparent in a modelling and shaping of the rest of the child's body, especially the limbs. And then it will be a question of treating each of these kinds of children, the cosmic and the earthly, in the right way.[55]

Interestingly, this characterization always relates to a connection with the child's body and soul nature, and refers to a particular temperament. For example, in describing the contrast between the child with a relatively large and relatively small head, he points to the phlegmatic and sanguine temperaments; and when he comes to the 'earthly' child he refers to a 'melancholic undertone' below the surface of the child's general temperament. If we study the children with a strong earthly disposition, we do indeed discover this melancholic undertone, though rarely as primary temperament.

Apart from significantly enriching our perceptions by employing this perspective, pedagogical aspects also come into play here. Souls with a cosmic predisposition need some help in learning about the world of reality; they have no special interest in the factual world, and one cannot simply give them unprepared access to this world. They most easily find their way into this domain through art. Here we must hearken to the pedagogical law that any material or subject must be artistically penetrated if it is to leave an impression in children's souls.

In this way, a task in arithmetic will only work upon the child if he finds that it relates to something real and important in the world. In other words, we need to pass from a description of an actual situation to the arithmetic process in question. With the more earthly children we can proceed in the opposite direction, starting from the mere fact of the task itself to its reality in the world. We will see that the more cosmic children take great pleasure in stories of all kinds whereas the more earthly ones attend more to actually occurring events. It is more or less self-evident that the former children have more affinity with the 'ensouled movement' of eurythmy, while the latter prefer sport and gymnastics.

Naturally these comments are not absolutes, but just soul dispositions that also manifest in the child's body. We should consider, though, that the culture in which we live today naturally has greater sympathy with the earthly as opposed to the cosmic orientation. The difference between these two dispositions consists in a polarity in the psyche, in the astral body, and we can see that children's interests acquire their direction or tendency from this (karmically determined) disposition. An eleven-year-old boy who is fascinated with computer games will certainly have brought with him a different bodily foundation than another of the same age who reads books day and night. A twelve-year-old girl who is obsessed with horses has a different bodily constitution from one wholly devoted to her clothes and their appearance. Pedagogy can to some extent broaden and balance such one-sided interests.

The relationship of the I to the body

The contrast between an I that is too deeply immersed in the body or too loosely connected with it is of great significance in our times. But first I'd like to highlight a possible misunderstanding. This contrast does *not* refer to the way in which a child incarnates at birth. Rather it concerns how the I itself (and *not* the I organization) relates to the body. The dynamic involved here is that of an I either too deeply drawn in by the body or too loosely connected with it. Is it possible for us to perceive this relationship?

In the contrast between cosmic or earthly orientation we were in the realm of the soul itself, whereas here we are in the realm of spirit, of the I. Steiner explained the perspective that led him to this way of seeing things in four lectures, given exactly a year after the school was founded. They appeared as CW 302a, under the German title of 'Meditatively acquired insights into the human being' and were regarded in fact as a kind of supplement to Steiner's basic educational courses. (A comparison between lecture two of *The Foundations of Human Experience* and lecture two of *Balance in Teaching* ['Meditatively acquired insights into the human being'] can provide astonishing confirmation of the scope of these added insights.)

In the last of these lectures, the relationship between the I and the body is explained in terms of the 'births' of physical body, etheric body and astral body 'anchoring the I in the whole human organism'. In other words, *development means the I taking hold of the child's corporeality, so that this I gradually comes to expression in the organism.*

If the I is sucked too deeply into the body this becomes apparent, for instance, in a thinking with marked affinity to material things: such thinking much prefers living in facts, in the world's realities. Anything clear and logical is preferred to things artistic and pictorial in nature. A soul of this kind finds it difficult to express itself artistically, or to dwell in reflective thoughts or a particular mood. Nor is listening to a story easy. As this individual approaches adulthood he will face the question of whether he works to live or lives to work. Here the I is a prisoner of the body, and physical functions and requirements overlay the quiet questions of the I. Enjoyment, rather than being a means to an end (see *Knowledge of the Higher Worlds*) becomes an end in itself. It is striking that Steiner regards this disposition as the basis for criminality.

If the I is too loosely connected with the body on the other hand, this gives rise to lack of direction and commitment; possibly also to idealism, but not to the extent of fully tangible, let alone realized ideals. Here we see the sentimentalist or utopian, full of good intentions that are forgotten as soon as uttered. The idea does not find its way into deed. Wonderful conversations are held but go no further. As an individual like this approaches adulthood he faces the question of what he should make of his life, what he is really there for. Steiner describes this one-sidedness as a 'theosophical' disposition. Here too we can see how topical such descriptions are in the contemporary world, bringing into sharp focus all the extremes of materialism and idealism apparent in our civilization, along with the vital importance of education itself.

In Steiner's verbal account, these phenomena are formulated in an absolute way, for he was speaking to an audience he knew well. If we modify these extremes into tendencies inherent in all of us (including ourselves as educators) we can also find ways to overcome or transform them. It seems to me an important step in self-knowledge to be able to find a tendency in one of these two directions in one's own constitution. Perceiving this in oneself, one has also taken an important step towards better pedagogy, for what I find within me is something I can make use of when I have the privilege of teaching children.

It is always astonishing how *subtle and delicate* Steiner's pedagogical suggestions are when he seeks to remedy a one-sided quality in a child's constitution. If there is a tendency for a pupil to be drawn too strongly into his body, Steiner recommends teaching in a way that can give him a strong, personal, pictorial relationship to the subject. The soul is stimulated and enlivened by this, and in turn communicates this to the I.

Where a child's I is too weakly connected with his body, the suggestion is to keep a certain distance from the subject matter, i.e. to remain more in the conceptual realm, for instance keeping mathematics in a more purely conceptual domain – though this too can be undertaken with strong inner engagement. This approach calls directly on the child's higher soul faculties. Steiner's text is not easy to fathom here, and so I offer the following explanatory table:

When the I needs to connect more strongly with the body:	When the I needs to connect less strongly with the body:
– arithmetic, mathematics, geometry and concepts of number and area	– more outward emphasis on geometrical drawings/ constructions
– everything in language and recitation that tends towards the musical and rhythmic	– in language giving more consideration to the content and meaning
– recall of musical elements, developing a tone memory (e.g. singing a melody both forwards and backwards)	– in music, placing less emphasis on memory and more on the immediate hearing experience

– everything of a mathematical nature in geometry (contour levels, cartography and suchlike)	– geography in general
– observing the conceptual element underlying things drawn or written	– all modelling and drawing
– observing how history is imbued with ideas; seeing the wider, overall context of events	– history in general; and developing a strong feeling participation in the events studied

Here, among other things, we have a description of the effect of modelling/sculpting forces on the one hand, and that of speech and music on the other. Steiner also gives examples of possible lessons. Pedagogues need to try to understand these effects and, where needed, employ this balance in their teaching, though not only with the aid of the examples given above. (For instance, a faculty of teachers could study the whole curriculum from this perspective.)

– Handwriting can be employed for both constitutions, that is, both for drawing the I into the body more (in observation of what has been written) and in loosening the I from the body (in the writing activity itself).

- The teaching of grammar will in general draw the I more strongly into the body.
- But inventing a grammar exercise oneself or playing a grammar game has a loosening tendency.
- Physics, where one observes and engages with an experiment, has a loosening effect.
- Studying theoretical physics and seeking general laws has a consolidating effect.
- In this regard, chemistry is similar to physics.
- The same is true of biology in the upper school: both loosening and consolidating effects can be employed in these subjects.
- Painting loosens. (This is why it is so healthy after the lesson to observe with children what they have painted, since this brings them back in.)
- Reading has a loosening effect, while reading aloud to others is stabilizing.
- Singing after reading draws the I back in: the children come back to themselves.
- Arithmetic has a consolidating and indrawing effect.
- Form drawing after arithmetic has a loosening effect.

If we study these four polarities or tendencies together, we must then ask how we can do justice to them in our observation and perception of the child. Steiner has a simple answer, and in giving it he touches at the same time on what one might call the Achilles heel of Waldorf education.

What is artistic teaching or the art of education?

In trying to shape our teaching artistically we can 'work upon' polarities and tendencies in the child and individually balance them. Here we encounter a secret of the effect of education as an artistic process which has so far not been wholly understood. And this gives rise in turn to the question we're very familiar with: What *is* artistic teaching? We all know how art affects us: the idea of enjoyment can give us initial access to this realm. What happens in us when we enter a museum – apart from the fact that our feet get tired after a couple of hours? One observation is that we have to direct a certain energy through our eyes in order to 'open up' our experience of a picture or sculpture. While this is a quite natural activity for some, others find it requires a good deal of effort. On emerging again, we feel as if we are still carrying the images around in our head. One can feel like a bee that has visited a flower, and now carries rich pickings in the head area. Gradually these experiences settle in us, and our senses acquire a new inner stability and structure. The soul sucks in the pictorial experiences, but does so largely in the neuro-sensory domain.

Or we attend a concert. There we sit and forget all about our body. We become all ears, and likewise 'forget' our breathing. We enter fully into the stream of tones in time, and feel how our soul resonates with it. Once the concert is over and we're outside in the street again, we still feel encompassed in a kind of tone cloud. We feel fully refreshed, in soul rather than body.

These are subtle feelings, but it is definitely worth trying to get hold of them and bring them to our awareness. If we bring the same sensitivity to bear on a monthly festival of children's work at school, where both modes of experience arise and meet, this is not only a rich experience but can also show us the pedagogical nature of art in education. It is of great significance to engage with such perceptions today. Teachers themselves so often doubt the need for artistic shaping of their subject matter, because they don't fully grasp the effect of this. How often, in Waldorf circles, is art used as an end rather than a means?

But if we seek to understand how the artistic element works in children and adolescents – in the polarities that have been described here – we will come one step nearer to realizing an art of education as this is needed today. In trying to do this we can also start to answer justified questions about the right degree of art in teaching. Questioning what is useful in this realm, and what is not, has a cleansing and inspiring potency for the whole way we approach teaching.

VII. CASE STUDIES

Introduction

Examples of child studies can give us insight into pedagogical practice. On the other hand, their disadvantage is that the example given might be used as some kind of template for similar situations. It can happen in child studies that as one listens one is reminded of other children who may bear a resemblance to the child under discussion. We need to remain alert here to ensure we retain the necessary openness in each different case. Anything suggested in one instance can only be valid for the particular child and situation. Something similar *might* be at work in another child, but this is usually fairly rare. Every child or adolescent contains his own unique riddle which it is our task to solve.

The following examples are all taken from actual practice, but have been anonymized. If a description strikes you as familiar this will not mean you have recognized a specific child, but only some familiar characteristics.

Frieda

A girl in the last year of kindergarten, small and delicately built. The school doctor reports that she was born ten days late. In her interactions with others she often raises her shoulders, making a tight impression. She has very blonde hair, blue eyes, a broad head with a high, wide forehead and a slightly snub nose. For her age, she has a rather critical glance. Frieda walks with a firm step and when she jumps does so 'heavily', in a way that seems very compact. Her motor skills are good, fluid and harmonious, and she follows through with her intentions.

Second dentition has already begun, and there is no doubt she is ready for 'big school'. The girl has tense, 'hard' muscle tone, likes salty foods and finds it hard to fall asleep. She is also ill quite often and then needs a long time to recover. When her older sister left kindergarten for Class 1, she too wanted to leave. There were big scenes lasting three weeks. Then a trainee kindergarten teacher from abroad appeared, whom you could tell came from a far-away land. The other children liked her very much for she was kind and sweet-natured; but Frieda developed such a fierce antipathy to her that she worked out strategies to avoid speaking with her, sitting next to her or having any contact at all with her. The child could play well otherwise, and was well-liked. However, when sharing lifts, she took care never to sit next to a certain girl who was generally not well-liked by the others. Her play is very creative but she almost always plays in the company of one particular girl and does not instigate contact with the children in her group, tending to withdraw from them. She can read. If you speak to her she won't look at you. She has a deep, strong voice and does not easily get over disagreements. Her mother says that when other children come to her house to play it always takes her an hour to adjust and be 'normal' again. When others visit she is at first very reticent. Her drawings and paintings show she is coming into her body well.

This sums up the first part of the child study.

What might the second stage of the study involve?
As mentioned, one might try to perceive the child's etheric and soul configuration, which would certainly lead to an outcome. But in this case, the chair of the meeting invited his colleagues to say what aspects of the phenomena they thought should be considered so as to lead to better understanding of the child. The following suggestions for further discussion were made:

– sympathy and antipathy
– forgetting/forgiving and harbouring grudges
– the child's (good) motor skills
– her social interactions
– (possible) anxieties
– her thoughts and way of thinking
– the contrast between her delicate build and the impression of heaviness

The meeting decided to focus on Frieda's thoughts and thinking, and anxieties that might be arising from this.

What do the raised shoulders tell us? And what the prematurely critical look?

This gesture seems the opposite of openness. Does it show that what the girl experiences in her surroundings coalesces into fixed thoughts which she can't get rid of again? (Holding grudges?) The heaviness in her jump does not result from physical heaviness, and her motor development is excellent. Are we seeing the burden or weight of her thoughts here? (As we know, for instance, the idea of visiting the dentist is usually worse than actually going.) What is the meaning of her difficulty in falling asleep? Usually this happens if the soul cannot release itself, often because the soul faculty of thinking is still stuck in its thoughts so that the soul bodies fail to disengage.

The girl has a strong will, is intelligent, and found ways of coping with her disposition until her sister no longer came to kindergarten after the summer holidays, at which she became defiant about going there too. What caused this?

Her broad head is a picture of the fact that she cannot easily relinquish ideas of how things should be. We see here a refusal that is astonishing for this age. The metabolism is too powerful in her head region. And then, when a trainee appears who does not fit in with her picture of things, she shuts off inwardly. Outwardly her behaviour becomes stand-offish and antipathetic, which largely originates in her fixed ideas. But when she is in a situation she knows, the same power of thinking and imagination becomes a positive attribute, as we can see in her gift for playing.

Frieda's strong power of thinking and picturing makes problems for her, and comes to expression in her behaviour. Her kindergarten teacher reports that she can communicate well with Frieda, even if the girl seems to speak into space rather than to her directly. Whenever a visitor comes, the child takes a while to get used to this and open up, since her inner thinking life is strong and does not easily let in something 'different'. We are therefore seeing here something approaching what Steiner calls a child with a strong imagination.

This gives us a hunch that we have found a key to understanding the child's soul, which would enable us to move on to the third part of the child study.

In this case, in fact, this turned out to be unnecessary. This was partly because the kindergarten teacher had found ways of helping the child, and partly because there are good grounds for believing that, when she moves to Class 1 and her thinking engages with more formal learning, these disturbances will be alleviated. The 'problem' with the trainee was resolved in the following way. With both the teacher and the trainee in the room, the latter began a game: all children put their shoes in a basket, and the trainee tried to guess which shoes belonged to whom. If she guessed correctly, she gave them to the owner, who could put them on and go out to play in the sunshine. The girl had the choice of either staying inside or going outside with everyone else. She chose the latter, and the ice was broken.

As we see here, an important aspect of these two first stages of the child study is that there is no need at all for any *moral judgement*.

Marcel

This child did not arrive at the Waldorf school until Class 4, coming because his 'needs could no longer be met' in his State primary school. He is the oldest of three brothers. Marcel is slim, of normal size, wiry, with a dark complexion. The back of his head is prominent and he has lively brown eyes that seem close together, and a big, broad mouth with strongly curving almost bulging lips. His mouth is usually open, he laughs a lot and has a deep somewhat rough voice. Marcel has previously broken an arm and a leg. His movements are quick, and he has dark-brown, almost black hair.

His legs, on closer examination, are those of a real boy – full of grazes, bruises and small wounds. He likes climbing trees, wades through streams in his gym shoes, and builds huts. In other words he is an 'outdoor child' by inclination. His favourite occupations are climbing trees and handball games. But his parents discipline him a great deal: the family places much emphasis on learning and good behaviour.

He has fitted in well with the rest of the class. Everyone likes him even if he sometimes really annoys his classmates. Although he easily makes contact with others, he does not have any firm (lasting) friend.

In lessons, Marcel is extremely provocative, and often involved in things that have nothing to do with the matter in hand. Wherever possible he distracts himself and others, ignores the teacher, and when taken to task replies indiscriminately either with the truth or some fabrication.

He is very intelligent, has a good educational grounding and can do maths without a problem. His handwriting is wobbly, but he expresses himself well and with some maturity in his schoolwork, and here is even a little ahead for his age. He can't sing: in other words, he 'drones' since he is unable to imitate or hold a note. He has no interest in playing an instrument, and handwork is very difficult for him – the results of this work look pretty unappealing. He seems to live 'in the periphery' rather than centred in himself. All the externalities of written work are a big effort for him, and he is as yet a long way from producing a 'beautiful' page in his main lesson books. However, he is charming and his behaviour, even if disruptive, is equally so. He finds it impossible to sit still, and yet he is described as a friendly boy with warm feelings. The teacher sums up by saying: 'He can't get what's in his head down into his hands,' and asks for some advice about getting more of a grip on Marcel's behaviour.

It is clear that Marcel is of a sunny, sanguine disposition and always retains his good mood through thick and thin. Wiry and slim, intelligent and agile, always engrossed in what is happening around him, and not very centred in himself. It is interesting that he has a strong gift for movement, but always in relation to his own games and not when he is meant to do something that doesn't fit in with his plans, such as playing the recorder. Then there is a (small) problem in relation to his inner attentiveness. A child who cannot sing because he can't 'find' the note usually does not have a problem with his ears but with his listening.

It seems that this question of internalization is generally perceptible in this otherwise very healthy, normal boy. His temperament and general constitution do not make it easy for him to internalize things; and yet he is regarded as intelligent, and has no learning difficulties. That is, the intellectual side of learning (which is also after all a form of internalization) functions very well. (Sanguine children, in fact, are rarely ungifted.) He needs help now in developing more capacity to internalize and dwell inwardly on things. Ritalin treatment is something one certainly wishes to avoid!

The following suggestions are made:

Firstly:
Each day a tone is struck on a glockenspiel (metallophone) without anyone seeing which tone it is. A little further away is another metallophone, and a pupil must try to find and strike the right tone at the first go. Marcel of course has a regular turn at this. The pupils can also try this themselves at break times. The teacher observes whether Marcel gradually learns to hear the right tone and strike it; and a second step would then be to see if greater success in listening can also benefit his singing.

Secondly:
Since Marcel did not join the Waldorf school until Class 4, it is suggested that he progressively catch up

with some of this work, starting with simple forms and quickly moving on to harder ones until he can master the difficult knotwork motifs. The idea is for him to do this over a four-week period and then leave it, and see how he develops. It would be best for this to happen in a separate one-to-one situation, perhaps with the remedial/support teacher.

Thirdly:
Each day he should try to write one sentence – and only one – as beautifully as possible in a book given him for this particular purpose. He is to do this at home and show it to the teacher every morning. A task for both the teacher *and* pupil! This is usually very effective.

Fourthly:
The teacher should react as little as possible to Marcel's disruptive behaviour; and when he does, with no hint of frustration or scolding but just gently and perhaps humorously correcting him. Review how things are after ten weeks.

Bruno

is in Class 4 and previously attended kindergarten. He has a sister three years older who is different from him in every way. His mother is worried about him because he seems so uninvolved and rarely shows joy in anything. Bruno is on the small side and chubby, and therefore seems a little ponderous. His gaze seems to look up at you from below and ask, 'Do you like me?' His large head is striking, with wavy blonde hair. His limbs, by contrast, seem inconspicuous. He is short sighted and wears glasses. Despite his fairly short legs his gait is sturdy, and he is more skilful at jumping than you would think. At break times outside he can run rings round other children without even noticing. He is rarely ill, and has an extremely good appetite.

He falls asleep early, sleeps long, and finds it difficult to get up in the morning.

He doesn't like taking part in the morning circle or rhythmic part of main lesson; and just as he can out-run other children, he can also be excessively sharp-tongued and verbally wounding to his classmates. His face does not give much away: it is almost as if he is unaware of his effect on others. In this class it is customary for children to learn their report verses by heart and to say them aloud on occasion, and therefore it is sometimes his turn to do this. He refuses to learn the verse by heart; and when it is said line by line for him to repeat, he does so with visible reluctance. He does not much like speaking at all, and it seems alien to him to engage with a class discussion, let alone to say anything himself. His class-teacher feels he has little interest in the subjects taught, and suspects that he also finds it hard to inwardly picture stories and other content.

He knows his times tables when they are recited rhythmically, but is stumped if asked, out of context, what 7 x 8 are. He likes copying from the board, but it is difficult for him to write something himself, and he will then copy from a neighbour. In the same way, when drawing in his main lesson book he 'borrows' ideas for pictures from the child next to him. Once he gets down to it he carries on until he has finished the task. Arithmetic is hard work for him. In break time play or organized games he shows little ability or grasp of what's happening, and when this leads to problems he seems completely unaware that he has caused them. His teacher finds him very unconfident and asks how one might free him up and 'waken' him. The year before, he had speech therapy, but this had little or no effect.

Here we see, therefore, a somewhat ponderous boy, certainly with a phlegmatic element. 'Ponderous' means here that the forces that formed the body have not yet relinquished their task in favour of intellectual pursuits. Steiner describes how school readiness means that the forces that formed the child's body are transformed into powers that can be used for learning. In Steiner's terms, growth forces become soul forces. This is the change that happens when children are ready for school – one that, in contrast to mainstream views, can happen fairly abruptly. In Bruno's case this process seems to have been delayed. What might be the cause of this?

To picture this process vividly we could say that the warmth pole is dominating the light pole. The metabolism is preventing the unfolding of intelligence.

Bruno is now reaching an age when he starts to notice that his classmates are different. But he can't get hold of himself since everything feels difficult, both his own body and the content of lessons, and also his relationships with his classmates. If one is unable to feel enthusiasm for anything, weight becomes heavier, for enthusiasm gives us wings.

We always need a balance between light and warmth. Here we can only suspect that the causes lie in the realm of pre-birth decisions or conditions. It may even be an important theme in his development to discover what gives 'light'. All his social capacities both now and later will depend on this. His lack of social competency does not lie in the social domain but in his unbalanced constitution between upper and lower poles.

How can we help him?

The following is suggested:

Firstly:
The glance that seeks affirmation should be answered by encouraging attentiveness. (This is often easier said than done, since such children do not immediately elicit sympathy.) Besides interest and attention from the class-teacher, all colleagues should be urged to offer him encouragement.

Secondly:
If the parents agree to this he should be woken earlier in the morning than he likes, and given a short, cold shower. If possible, his clothing should be light rather than too warm. His lack of participation in the morning circle should be accepted for now, but instead of that he will need to respond daily in a 5-minute class session of mental arithmetic (the teacher can take him

aside and confidentially tell him that he will need to do this each day). Round singing in Class 4 can offer an opportunity for, say, a three-part round with two children in each part (6 children) and then with only three pupils, ensuring that Bruno is often one of those in this last group of three.

Thirdly:
In a separate book kept at home, every day Bruno should do five times table sums that the teacher gives him, and make up five more of his own that he also works out the answer to. He should carry on doing this for several months, and they should be of increasing difficulty. This will also require persistence on the teacher's part.

It is likely that other children may want this kind of homework after a while. If this happens, this will be the very best outcome since then Bruno's own enthusiasm will have connected with the other children, and in turn work back on him again, making the atmosphere 'light and bright'. This is the secret of an approach to arithmetic not pursued for the sake of marks.

Fourthly:
At some point and by some means or other, the class-teacher must discover something that Bruno is interested in and introduce this into her lessons. This might take a while, but persistence should eventually be rewarded. If Bruno has a field of interest and this can be skilfully introduced into lessons, he could be a transformed child in a few months. The age of 9 to 10 has this quality: great changes can arise from little impetus.

After eight to ten weeks the teachers should review any progress and changes. Have we been able to help?

Nathalie

We saw Nathalie near the end of Class 1. Before that she had been in the kindergarten at the same school for two years, and already had something of a reputation when she got here. Nathalie looks delightful, rather like a small, dark-eyed gypsy. She is slim, agile, has long black eyelashes, long black hair and seems aware of her appearance despite being only just 8 now. When she was in Class 1 her parents has a baby boy, her brother. Both her parents are artists and do not find parenting easy.

She eats normally, with no special preferences, but she finds it hard to fall asleep. She stays awake for ages, and has lots of dreams and nightmares, and then wakes up crying and shouting. On these occasions her parents are not sure if she is really fully awake, since she also sometimes sleep-walks – not regularly, but a few times a year. In kindergarten Nathalie was an open and affectionate child, but was able to set the girls, especially, against each other in the twinkling of an eye, leaving the teacher standing there helpless. She apportioned her favours as she chose, decided who would play with whom, and who was to be excluded from a game. In other words, she was a law unto herself. In Class 1 this continued at break times in the playground. There was scarcely a break time any more without some big drama. Peace only reigned if she stayed in at break, which was clearly not a long-term solution. It frequently happened that her father brought her to school an hour late, because of a dispute about which dress she was going to wear. In such instances she was overpoweringly headstrong. Classmates who were in favour one day would find they had been excluded the next, causing continual upsets in the class community.

Yet Nathalie is also a pleasant child, intellectually and above all artistically gifted. Her way with colours when drawing and painting, and the way she sets out her written work, all bear witness to maturity and talent. She developed a great facility for drawing Barbie dolls, like a comic-strip artist: always with the same stereotype stances and gestures, but in an ever-varying wealth of colours. This was very skilful but somewhat one-sided. When stories were told to the class she became a 'little girl' again: thumb in mouth, losing herself completely in the story. Nathalie is graceful, skilled with her hands, sociable and willing to help. If you see her in the classroom you cannot believe what happens at break times.

The class-teacher asked for help because of the problematic nature of her headstrong will.

We saw before us a lovely girl, the epitome of artistic in everything she did, and this already at the end of Class 1. There was something elegant yet mannered about her movements, similar to the Barbie drawings she did – as if she had practised her poses before the mirror.

Her handwriting on the other hand was strong and individual, and her knitting in handwork was colourful and well-made. She learned everything easily and effortlessly, both reading and numbers. In eurythmy, one could discern not only her gift for movement but also her internalization of the movements, and her strongly expressive capacity. Nathalie is a very healthy child with many gifts, and it seems quite possible that an artistic talent will develop.

But where do these remarkable outbreaks of anger come from when choosing her dresses, and these strange social tensions? If one observes Nathalie in the playground one sees that she does not intend to be divisive. The trouble already starts as she allocates roles in games. Having set the cat among the pigeons, she does not withdraw from the tumult but joins in vigorously.

The impression one is left with is that she has no wish to cause divisions between her classmates, but something provokes this in her.

And what about sleep? What is the general significance of sleep for a child?

Most people will notice that broken sleep has repercussions for how you feel next day. You don't feel fully there – not only tired but irritable. Mothers with babies waking up at night know all about this! Strong individuals cope relatively well with this and can draw on their reserves of energy, but more sensitive natures find it harder. Is it possible that Nathalie's arguments with her parents about what clothes to wear in the morning could be the result of sleep deprivation? Is the sleep problem too much for her?

Is it possible that the day 'slips out of her grasp' like good sleep does, and pushes her into forms of social interaction that she does not actually intend, but that have acquired their own momentum through her strong character and temperament? Whoever sleeps badly at night can't wake up properly during the day.

But why does Nathalie sleep badly? Is it because her somewhat prematurely developed soul finds it hard to 'switch off' in the evening? Are the impressions of the day working in her too strongly?

In that case, shouldn't the impressions received by this receptive soul be softened or attenuated? To the question of whether she appears overwrought one has to say that she both does and doesn't. In her school-work and when listening to stories she certainly isn't wound up, but very focused. When playing with other children, something else comes into the picture.

The following suggestions are made:

Firstly:
The parents should introduce a different bed-time ritual: a quiet evening, then a story and warm milk with honey, followed by a brief conversation about everything nice that happened that day; and then bed.

Secondly:
The school doctor suggested a warm stomach compress or – if that was too much trouble – a hot water bottle on the stomach. If the metabolism receives a little help, is given a little treat, with warm, sweet milk and com-

press, the neuro-sensory pole will find it easier to let the metabolism take over, or in other words fall asleep.

The parents (who were receptive to this since they were worried about the situation) were also asked to record whether the sleep interruptions improved, and whether there was a connection between the tantrums in the morning and the quality of sleep.

Thirdly:
If these measures do not help, the school should let Nathalie have a little nap at break times in the kindergarten bedroom, even if this means she comes a little bit late to her next lesson.

Fourthly:
Teachers on break time duty should be sensitive to these circumstances, and aware of what happens in the playground. (In fact this also helped show that the whole school should be more aware of the responsibilities of break supervision.)

After eight to ten weeks a review of progress. Have we done what we agreed, and what effect has it had?

In this case a really sensational improvement occurred. After a few weeks Nathalie had begun to sleep well, and her problems faded entirely.

(One thing we learned from this was that a problem is *almost always* a symptom. That is, in this case the social turbulence was not connected with the child's lack of social ability but related to her constitution.)

John

John has attended the Waldorf school from the beginning of his school days and is now entering Class 12.

He comes from a well-educated family, has two younger siblings; and a decision is needed now about whether he should be allowed to take his school-leaving exams (Abitur).

John is tall and slim, has smooth, dark blonde hair and light blue eyes. His complexion is usually pale, his features and mouth narrow. He holds his head a little to one side and walks with a shuffling gait. He always tips his chair while sitting, balancing there while he wraps his (thin) legs around the chair legs. He can also balance the chair on one leg and spin right round on it in a flash to see everyone else in the class. He spends most of his time at school playing some invented game or one he has brought with him from home. Occasionally – though rarely – he can suddenly let fly at a classmate for no known reason.

His engagement with school subjects in general is consistently poor. His handwriting is small and well-formed, and all regard him as intelligent.

He is excellent at maths and Latin, and in history (in which he usually doesn't participate) he can suddenly come up with an answer that hits the nail on the head. If he's in the mood, he can fill a whole lesson with unsolicited interjections which always precisely home in on something (usually embarrassing). As the teachers humorously put it, he has a great talent for nonsense. He's always ready to throw in a comical, jokey or absurd comment. He is also a quick thinker, and a born 'minimalist': his main lesson books are distinguished by their yawning voids. But if you ask him to speak about some complex theme in physics, he can do this without a pause or preparation, without notes, and always correctly and brilliantly.

He is described as being sharp as lightning, with a pronounced aversion to anything musical. His movements in eurythmy are weak and inexpressive, but he is excellent at sport. The music teacher says he has never heard him sing but has seen him do so – as if ashamed. He will only take part in a play if the performance is sure not to take place during the holidays. He rarely looks at a teacher. In modelling and sculpture he is an outstanding pupil: all his work in this field is very expressive, and the same is true of his drawing.

His (large) class supports him with loving indulgence. Classmates like him pretty well although his idiosyncrasies have led to some discord amongst parents ('he ought to be thrown out')!

And there is another thing: he has an angelic and almost girlish face (simply a factual description). And for years he has been faithfully helping a less gifted fellow pupil with his homework: every day consistently. A further distinctive trait is that he won't drink alcohol.

The teachers say that of course he ought to take the exams since he is perfectly intelligent, and yet large gaps have arisen in his education. What should be done?

Here we had, therefore, a tall, slim young man who likes to balance on his chair as he wraps his legs around it, rather than sitting solidly on it. It seems as if his intelligence drives him forward without him forming a real relationship with any subject. Then there is his endless enjoyment of jokes, humour and jest. (Here we could ask what humour or jest really are. They arise, surely, when one does not fully connect with something but stays a little detached, an observer, at one remove. Humour rarely appears when we are fully immersed in a situation. We only see the comical side of things when we regard them from outside.)

We can have the sense that this young man is standing outside *everything*. He is not grounded or really connected with things. Someone who has reached the age of 18 without any sign of his life so far being inscribed on his face, remains free and has not yet (to use Steiner's term for puberty) entered upon 'earth maturity'. (During the study, no mention was made, either, of any girlfriend.) There are many pupils today who, due to the nature of our culture, get too immersed in 'earthly maturity', sometimes causing significant problems, also of a moral nature. John by contrast tends to be too 'light', or one might also say 'ideal'.

Steiner, as we have seen, makes a distinction between a soul configuration that can either be too cosmic or too earthly; and this is the contrast, really, that I have just referred to. In this young man's whole figure, behaviour and lack of pursuit and development of his intelligence, we see an 'upward' orientation and evasion. He *possesses* intelligence but he has not yet made much *of it*.

Phenomena that don't seem to fit with the rest of the picture are especially interesting since they can often indicate the solution to the riddle, or the way forward. What has given rise to his apparently untypical engagement with sculpture and his genuine talent for drawing? Is it this that satisfies his need to connect with the world? We also heard about his skills in sport although one wouldn't have thought this from his figure.

Are these the ways he relates to the world? And perhaps also by regularly helping his friend?

Is it possible that we have a very beautiful, gifted soul here, who as yet is prevented from fully entering into life?

His etheric and soul (astral) configuration are very rich. But after puberty the astral body has not developed into a bearer of the will, of the I. He is still hovering. How can we help him?

The following suggestions are made:

Firstly:
He should have a mentor who communicates to him the will of the faculty of teachers that he *must* take his Abitur (if you like as therapy, though that won't be said to him). If he fails miserably that is up to him; but the faculty wants to help and support him.

Each Friday his mentor should review the week with him, seeing what went well and what didn't. The mentor will support him in bringing *awareness to bear on his life* by urging him to keep a diary – as a kind of record of what ran smoothly in relation to schoolwork, and what didn't. In which lessons did he succeed in paying attention and participating?

(At this point it was objected that the staff did not have the time for this. My reply was as follows: If a school seeks quality, this argument is irrelevant, for one has to set real priorities. And this case has priority. One could also say that the school has left things very late in the day before acting.)

Secondly:

If possible the mentor will (if he cannot do this himself) send John to the literature teacher who will recommend some important biographies for him to read *alongside* his other schoolwork. It would be good if he could give some presentations on this reading. These would be biographies that describe how someone has been battered by fate yet ultimately triumphs over his adversities. It would be good if the mentor and John could discuss his reading and related thoughts on the Friday afternoons when they meet. In this way the mentor will also be helping John to practise trust and communication in their conversations. (There really is no end to suitable biographies. A few titles: *A Part of Myself, Portrait of an Epoch* (by Carl Zuckmeyer), *Mein Leben* ('My Life', by Emil Nolde), *Geliebtes Sibirien* ('Beloved Siberia', by Traugott von Stackelberg), *Three Cups of Tea* (by Greg Mortenson), *The Glass Castle* (by Jeanette Walls) and many more.

For a certain period John can be supported by having a 'substitute I' in the form of a mentor; but this will only work if the mentor takes this young man seriously, and lets him see that he, the mentor, really wants to support him and help things move forwards.

Thirdly:
If John can see that people genuinely wish to stand by him, then one can also tell him there are certain eurythmy therapy exercises that can help him to strengthen his connection with the world. If he can recognize the value of this and find enough trust, he should do eurythmy therapy exercises that connect the upper and lower astral body, so that the latter in turn engages more strongly with his life forces.

Fourthly:
All upper school teachers who have anything to do with John should undertake to show a supportive rather than a critical attitude towards him. It is possible this might even enable him to start singing, for singing means being present at the centre of one's soul; and it is difficult to sing if one doesn't find this centre.

Every six weeks, in their meeting, the faculty of upper school teachers should review how John is doing. (There is always time for something one is genuinely interested in.)

Milan

Milan attends Class 9 at a large Waldorf school, which he joined in Class 3 when he and his parents arrived from eastern Europe. He has a sister who is four years younger than him. When Milan was 12, his father returned to his native country.

Milan is a sturdy young fellow – his strong musculature is apparent from a distance. When younger he was a cheerful rascal, and his skilled teachers managed to get him to learn what was necessary, though no more than that. Basically he was doing OK. His mother had attended the Waldorf school when she was young, and sent him there when she returned to Germany. His health is good. He was always well-liked, and full of ideals and big hopes (for instance he wanted to be a Formula 1 driver).

Milan's life has changed since the departure of his father (whom he worshipped and adored). He became introvert and completely gave up on his schoolwork (which he didn't much care for anyway). He started to disengage from the rest of the class. For a while people thought these were just the normal difficulties of puberty and were very lenient with him. Under much pressure from Milan, his mother gave in and let him buy a computer with internet access, with money he had earned himself; and then he began to spend more and more time in his room, where he had set up the whole thing. His mother stood by helplessly as she increasingly lost contact with Milan. He would spend long hours at night on the computer, then try to catch up on sleep at school. Teachers tried to help him by talking with his mother and eurythmy therapy, but his behaviour continued to deteriorate. He avoided his classmates and became aggressive if anyone asked anything of him. He also said things that could be interpreted as suicidal. He was accepted into the upper school under strict conditions, and it soon became obvious that his work was inadequate in every area.

The faculty was close to asking Milan to leave the school; and it was under these circumstances that the child study was held.

We saw before us a somewhat chubby lad with healthy but fairly pale skin. A growth spurt has begun. His gait is gangly and awkward, and the seat of his trousers seems to be almost between his knees. He is usually alone. His figure is neither athletic nor plump but somewhere between the two. The hairline of his short-cut, dark-brown hair comes noticeably far down his forehead. His ears are small and appear slightly flattened, and his neck is short. He has strong hands and a voice in the middle of breaking – sometimes low, sometimes high. Photos of him when he was younger reveal a cheerful boy with open mouth. He often suffered from colds and always had moisture around his nose and mouth. Otherwise he was a healthy child.

According to school reports, the decline in his work began in Class 7 and never recovered. The only subject where something positive can be said is in games. Thus a classic picture of puberty – if it were not for a sense that his lowered eyes and solitude convey something more than just pubescent behaviour. When asked about his behaviour he responds with phrases like, 'There's no point anyway', or 'Why should I learn this shit?' or 'Get off my back'. He appears to have turned inwards completely and to find every external approach a troublesome nuisance. His favourite phrase is 'Leave me alone'.

The impression we had was of a boy who has sunk entirely into himself and into gravity. He seems to regard any talk or idea as endlessly abhorrent, and all learning and thinking for the sake of it, as painful. But with computer games he has developed a swift reactive thinking and action. These pose no challenge for him however. Their ever-repeating sequences make few demands on him.

In speaking of too deep an immersion of the I in the physical body, Rudolf Steiner also remarks that one can notice this first in a person's thinking, which soon feels an affinity only with logical, material ideas, becoming one dimensional, superficial and mundane. If education does not counteract this, the soul and spirit (or the I) can be imprisoned by the body, which comes to govern wishes, longings and desires.

One can meet adolescents quite different in nature from our Milan, who will not be much harmed by a passing addiction to computer games. But in the case of someone like Milan this can become dangerous since he is in a situation (loss of his father, stressed mother, loneliness, no friends or hobbies) where he has nothing to counteract his games addiction. In this situation the computer can become a menace, as we have seen in recent tragedies in Erfurt, Winnenden, Oslo and America.

If Milan were in Class 5 one would try to use artistic activities to engage him, but this can no longer be done in Class 9. During the conversation, his class mentor reported a discussion about Milan with the chemistry teacher who said he was actually a nice pupil who doubtless had gifts, though it was hard to know what they were.

This remark led to a suggestion for the next chemistry main lesson for Milan's class. The chemistry teacher was asked if he could, as an experiment, demonstrate a developmental sequence in chemistry accompanied by the concepts corresponding to it, thus showing how reality can be grasped in ideas (specifically: how ether develops from starch, passing from potato through sugar to alcohol and ether, along with consideration of the associated foods, alcohols and analgesics). He was also asked if he could do this with Milan especially in mind, and during the main lesson present additional sequences of ideas tangibly demonstrated in experimental metamorphoses and transformations, inviting the students to conceptualize these sequences. It was fortunate that the teacher in question was very positive about this 'secret mission' and set to work energetically to realize it: to do something focused on one particular pupil which would also of course benefit the whole class community. Here the lesson material, involving a developmental sequence of chemical phenomena that could elicit conceptual engagement and activity, was set against the computer's merely mechanical, logical thinking.

Further to this, the eurythmy therapist and the eurythmy teacher sat down together and found themes for the eurythmy lessons involving the practice of rising melodic sequences, with strong alternation between minor and major keys. As Milan's mentor, the eurythmy therapist undertook to concern herself with him as intensively as possible, both through her interest in and commitment towards him, and in conversation with him.

Thus, in the second stage of the study already, we were full of ideas and intended actions. At the same time we remained anxious and realistic. Was it possible to help Milan? Could we open him up to the world, to learning, and to his own developmental potential?

We made a strong resolve to help him; but due to the uncertainty of the situation, we agreed to review successes and failures in the very near future.

In the following period, it seemed that something miraculous had happened. After the child study the young man appeared transformed in school. The chemistry main lesson achieved precisely what we had hoped for. Milan engaged well with the committed chemistry teacher and the lessons, and this contact continued after the main lesson ended. His mentor helped him to organize his schoolwork. His mother was told that he had turned over a new leaf, and his whole being and behaviour changed so much that it did indeed seem miraculous. With the least possible means we had achieved an unpredictably beneficial effect.

Jaimy

Jaimy is a thin, small, alert boy with blonde hair, swift in his movements and still swifter in his comments. Until Class 1 he attended a Catholic kindergarten but had problems there, which is why his parents sent him to the Waldorf school. Jaimy's parents are both successful in the world of business. A sister was born when Jaimy was four.

Now in Class 3, Jaimy is very agile and mercurial. When he started school he was still wetting the bed at night so much that he had to wear nappies. This problem has been resolved through intensive eurythmy therapy. He often has a cold and an ear infection.

As stated, Jaimy's speech and thought is very nimble too. He seeks his teacher's attention by saying such things as 'No time for me at the moment?' Or: 'Mr. Empel, that's right is it, I can't help at the moment can I?' When a story is told, say the one about Cain and Abel, he might shout out in the middle, 'But God sees everything, how can he let that happen?' He makes big demands on himself and is inconsolable if his drawings or writing don't meet his strict standards. The teacher has to find creative ways to divert him from this regret; or else he has to let him do the whole thing all over again. But this can mean digging a deeper hole, since the second or third version of a drawing may still not be perfect. Remarkably, Jaimy is unable to walk or clap rhythmically but he seems not to notice *this* particular problem.

Jaimy doesn't have any firm friends in the class. He

is quite well-liked but the other children are also a little afraid of him and uncertain towards him.

He is extremely skilled with his hands, and handwork is therefore his favourite lesson. His work in this subject really is above average; and he is also good at reading and arithmetic. He demonstrates a strange fluctuation between extremes: either he is very dreamy, engages with lessons as if sleepwalking; or he is over-alert. In the latter case he can be very disruptive, argues with the teacher, insults other children, hits out, scratches and is quite beside himself. The only thing that can help at such times is to send him out of the classroom and – if she's there – take him to the handwork teacher. Then he calms down immediately. He can hardly bear eurythmy: he throws himself on the ground and stays there.

The class-teacher is asking for help because sending him out of the room is not a long-term solution.

In terms of constitution, Jaimy must be ready for formal schooling: his learning ability and manual skill show that the part of the ether body responsible for this has taken up its proper task. However, the part of the ether body that governs bodily processes along with the astral body is not wholly integrated, as we can see from the bedwetting and the susceptibility to colds and ear infections. We see a weakness of the lower system (though cured in eurythmy) and of the upper system (manifesting in colds, which are displaced metabolic processes).

This relative weakness is reflected in his behaviour.

Either he is too awake or too 'sleepy'. When too awake he cannot sustain this, and does not cope with it since it does not connect with his metabolism. A task not successfully accomplished then appears to him as a life-threatening problem. Intensification of alertness becomes apparent in his frantic episodes. (Here once again we have an opportunity to remember never to judge such behaviour in moral terms. However much we may incline in this direction, to do so is an injustice to the child. His behaviour is *always the expression* of a situation that he cannot deal with.) If we consider Jaimy's physical form, we can perhaps already sense the problem. It is apparent that the head system has little connection with his limbs, with his metabolism. This results in the inability of such children to 'live out of their centre'. Their constitution is polarized, and so also their behaviour.

It ought really to be possible to balance this through normal, healthy Waldorf education. But in Jaimy's case the picture is a little too one-sided. He has the kind of constitution we can see in many children today, apparent among other things in difficulties with developing normal friendships. One should *not* say they have no social skills; but rather that something is *preventing* them from engaging in social contact. The difference is a big one as regards our stance towards a child.

Jaimy has a special gift which we may be able to build on: his manual dexterity. This can offer the very thing he needs to gain more equilibrium.

The following is suggested:

Firstly:
If possible he should eat something sweet after every meal. His stomach should feel comfortable. Hot foods are less good. It would be excellent if he could have a warm, sweet porridge for breakfast. (It wasn't clear from the conversation whether this would be possible at home.)

Secondly:
Women on the faculty find the boy easier than the men. He may lack motherly warmth. Can the class-teacher do more to create this mood in the classroom?

Thirdly:
The class-teacher should always have some ongoing project for the class involving manual skills. For instance, at break time some boys might be allowed to stay in and build a tall tower of Kapla blocks. Or, as class activity for a quarter of an hour each day, the children could make paper origami animals, or practise cat's cradle shapes with string. Then Jaimy will gain beneficial recognition in the class. If he's at risk of going overboard, he can be given an origami task that he can manage but is too difficult for the rest of the class. This will calm him down without him having to leave the room.

After eight to ten weeks the situation should be reviewed to see how things have gone and what has been effective.

Deborah

A small, delicate girl at the end of Class 1. She is dainty and agile, has blonde hair, is swift in her movements but unerring in everything she does.

During the mother's pregnancy, the child kicked and kept moving around almost every day after the seventh month, sometimes painfully so. After she was born, there were feeding and metabolic problems that now seem to have settled. The child has always had a sensitive skin, leading quickly to all kinds of allergies, though this is now easing.

She stood up and began to walk on her first birthday. She learned to speak early, uttering whole sentences when she was one-and-a-half; and by the age of two could argue articulately if she wanted something.

She is the second youngest in the class, and now has a younger brother.

When her mother brings her in the morning, the class-teacher can hear her issuing instructions about how she (the mother) must behave: no goodbye kiss, hold her satchel like this, please collect me on time etc. She never glances back as her mother leaves. She attended the kindergarten that belongs to the school, and we hear that there were difficulties.

When her mother has left, she throws herself on the class-teacher and clings to her, not letting go again until she has to. When the teacher succeeds in releasing her hold with much persuasion and encouragement, the child pushes her table and chair very close up to the teacher's so that she won't lose sight of her for the rest of the day. If possible she clings to her again at break time.

The teacher has the definite impression that this behaviour has more to do with a need to control than with any compensation for emotional neglect at home (which does not seem to exist).

Deborah has social difficulties. She is unable to play with other children. She also avoids looking directly at the teacher or classmates. She has long, slender hands and delicate fingers. If possible she will avoid shaking anyone's hand. Her movements, however, are very skilful. She is the best at rope-skipping. Skipping with two ropes swung in opposite directions gives her real pleasure, and one can tell this only by the fact that she will go on doing it endlessly rather than by any actual expression of pleasure.

In Class 1 she learned everything very quickly: reading and writing are easy for her. She prefers arithmetic however, and she always asks the teacher for difficult sums, at school and to take home. She likes drawing and painting, and does so imaginatively. (And likewise has an imaginary friend and playmate whom she calls 'my friend no one'.) There are colours that she doesn't like, though, yellow for instance, and she has broken the crayon of this colour in half and thrown it away. When she does wet-in-wet painting however, all the colours run into a mess together, leaving water and paint dripping off her board and making her furious.

She sometimes talks to herself, in quiet speech that can't be understood. But if you address her or if she is asked to tell or explain something to the class, her speech is significantly clearer. In these circumstances she has no inhibitions about expressing herself to the room in general. She argues with other children but has no ordinary conversations with them since she does not communicate with her classmates. She loves knitting, has piano lessons and enjoys them very much, and according to her mother sleeps soundly. Her parents are immigrants and she has been raised in two languages.

When her mother comes to fetch her in the afternoon, she leaves school without comment or greeting, orders her mother to get in the car, and goes.

In some child studies one ends up speechless for a while after the first part.

There is something evident here that occurs more or less in every child study: we don't know what the next step is; we feel helpless. What should we do? Where can we draw ideas for understanding a child like this and helping her?

It cannot be emphasized strongly enough how important this sense of helplessness is, this not knowing.

It is the narrow, painful doorway to inspiration. But you have to endure it. There are no certainties. In this kind of work one has to learn to stand before the void and endure it – deal with the fact that any answers, any solution to the riddle, cannot be gained by some clear procedure.

One therefore requires a certain courage too in staying with this work and not succumbing to doubt when uncertainty holds sway to start with.

If you don't cope with this uncertainty you will

instead reach for a system, a guideline, that inevitably leads you in a certain direction. That is one possibility. The other is that you listen to the problems and capitulate – in other words go no further than their characterization.

What we try to do, by contrast, is square the circle by finding a path in a pathless terrain.

If we allow the description of this delicate girl to work upon us, what stirs in us? On the one hand we see her delight in learning, and the way she goes towards the world fearlessly in this realm: her quick grasp of things, her joy in knitting, skipping, her hunger for arithmetic.

On the other, one feels a mild sense of oppression. How much tact the teacher has needed already to stop the girl clinging to her when, for instance, she talks to a colleague at break. One has to ask whether this clinging to the teacher expresses a need for emotional warmth or whether it reveals an anxiety about connecting with the world and other people. We felt that this was the really decisive question here.

This is because we need to know whether we have a case of emotional neglect before us (very common indeed, and often hidden as we know) or instead a picture from the autistic spectrum.

The child had metabolic disorders and a susceptibility to allergies in infancy. In autism research some investigators have found strange metabolic incongruities. There is no scope here to consider this in depth; one would have to enquire further.

What do the skin problems and allergies tell us? We

easily forget that the skin is also an organ, the largest we have. It has the unusual dual function of defending, protecting, and at the same time breathing. It is, if you like, a physical expression of our relationship to the world.

But we also heard that these problems are fading without medical intervention.

We are also wary, since the child is only just at the end of Class 1, of wading in with big measures. We would prefer to affirm and support the class-teacher in her difficult task of helping the child make contact with her classmates. All of us sensed some deep riddle in the relationship between the mother and daughter.

Now this school is very fortunate in having a eurythmy therapist, who suggested practising three consonants for a certain period, and then possibly repeating this again at a later stage, carefully observing any effect. He recommended (and was happy to do this himself with the child) G, L and M.

G creates inner space, and allows the world to be as it is. L, connecting above with below, sets processes in motion, releases rigidities, brings things into flow. Finally the M enables me to meet the world and internalize it, so that I can be in the world and the world in me.

The meeting adjourned with the intention of doing this at the beginning of Class 2. We wanted to leave it entirely up to the class-teacher to see if she might find an opportunity to speak to Deborah's mother about the child. We all felt that tact was needed with this mother-daughter relationship. In the autumn we would review how things had progressed following eurythmy therapy and the further work of the class-teacher.

References

Translator's note: CW 300 volumes cited below refer to the three volumes in German of *Konferenzen mit den Lehrern der Freien Waldorfschule in Stuttgart* (English: Faculty Meetings with Rudolf Steiner, two volumes). I have retranslated all Steiner passages quoted in this book.

NOTES

1 CW 300 c. Meeting on 15 July 1924
2 CW 293
3 CW 300 a. Meeting of 26 September 1919
4 CW 300 a. Meeting of 23 September 1920
5 CW 300 b. Meeting of 20 June 1922
6 CW 300 c. Meeting of 15 July 1924
7 J.W. Goethe, *Naturwissenschaftliche Schriften* vol. 5, p. 563, R. Steiner Verlag
8 R. Steiner, *The Christmas Conference for the Foundation of the General Anthroposophical Society* 1923–1924, CW 260
9 CW 300 c. Meeting of 5 February 1924
10 Address by Rudolf Steiner on 20 August 1919, as reconstructed by Erich Gabert in *Zur Vertiefung der Waldorfpädagogik*, Verlag am Goetheanum
11 CW 300 b. Meeting of 28 October 1922
12 See note 3 above
13 CW 300 c. Meeting of 28 October 1922
14 See the letter of farewell in *Zur Vertiefung der Waldorfpädagogik,* 2008, Dornach, Pedagogical Section
15 CW 310, *Human Values in Education*, lecture 5, Arnheim 21 July 1924
16 See CW 300 a, 14 June 1920
17 *The Foundations of Human Experience*, CW 293, lecture 1, Stuttgart 20 August 1919
18 In regard to the disastrous effect of specialization in schools, cf. *Geisteswissenschaftliche Behandlung sozialer und pädagogischer Fragen*, GA 192, lecture 2, Stuttgart

23 April 1919. In Steiner's view, the teacher is always first and foremost a pedagogue and only then a specialist in his field. Cf. *Human Values in Education*, CW 310, lecture 5, Arnheim 21 July 1924

19 Cf. Karl-Martin Dietz: *Arbeiten zur dialogischen Schulführung. Leben im Dialog, Perspektiven einer neuen Kultur,* Menon 2004

20 CW 295, *Seminar Discussions*, lecture 1

21 CW 300 a. Meeting of 9 June 1920

22 Although little use is made of the temperaments nowadays, a considerable body of secondary literature does exist on their origin and action:

1. Yona McDonough, *The Four Temperaments,* Arrow Books, 2003
2. Rudolf Steiner, *The Four Temperaments,* Rudolf Steiner Press, 2008
3. Stephen Montgomery, *People Patterns; A Modern Guide to the Four Temperaments,* Prometheus Nemesis Press, 2002

23 In particular, see two accounts by Steiner which, when compared with each other, present us with a particular challenge. In his moving farewell cycle of lectures in Stuttgart (CW 308, *The Essentials of Education*) Steiner describes the later effects of long-term exposure to a one-sided temperament. Immediately after these lectures, he travels to Bern and there also discusses this theme (CW 309, *The Roots of Education*). In Stuttgart the later effects of long-term exposure to the choleric temperament in childhood are ascribed to metabolic disorders, whereas in Bern they are ascribed to circulatory disorders.

24 This refers to the full account of health aspects in the art of education in CW 300 b, meeting of 6 February 1923, which is also a kind of key passage for understanding how pedagogical work can affect pupils' general health. In this

context, and only here, the idea of large- and small-head-edness is introduced.

25 Ibid

26 R. Steiner, *The Foundations of Human Experience*, CW 293, lecture 6, Stuttgart 27 August 1919

This diagram is important for the child study, since in every such study a moment of blankness comes: of not knowing how to continue. We face the void. Since we are highly programmed to avoid or evade such moments, we possess within us a mechanism that suppresses this facing of the void. And yet such moments are of the very greatest importance. Only by enduring our lack of knowledge, our inability to get further, can we find the gateway to inspiration and perhaps also even intuition. It is like a birth: a great deal of pain accumulates; but by enduring this we create a new quality, a new, inwardly secured knowledge. I will return to this theme in the last child study example.

27 Otto Scharmer, *Theorie U. Von der Zukunft her führen*. Carl Auer Verlag, Heidelberg 2009

28 R. Steiner, *Practical Advice to Teachers*, GA 294, lecture 1, Stuttgart 21 August 1919

29 This means that if all developmental deviations – from which normal development ultimately emerges – are compiled, 96% of all childhood development should be regarded as normal. In: Professor H. G. Schlack (ed.): *Entwicklungspädiatrie*, Hans Marseille Verlag, Munich 2004

30 The KIGGS survey ran again from 2009 to 2012, and further differentiated the original findings. See the online website of the Robert Koch Institute (RKI).

31 This trend has increased markedly in Germany in recent years: private schools (thus primarily Waldorf schools) have become a catch-all for pupils who can't cope with the state system, and this has a knock-on effect on the proportion of 'healthy Waldorf students'.

32 CW 307, 14 August 1923, Ilkley

33 For instance, CW 309, *The Roots of Education*, lecture 1, Bern 13 April 1924

34 In: *Aus Meinem Leben*, Urachhaus Verlag, Stuttgart

35 *The Foundations of Human Experience*, lecture 4, CW 293

36 Ibid

37 CW 293

38 *The Foundations of Human Experience*, lecture 2: '... the idea, the picture is sub-real while the will germ is super-real.'

39 *The Foundations of Human Experience*, lecture 4

40 *Balance in Teaching*, CW 302 a

41 *Modern Art of Education*, CW 307, lecture 10, Ilkley 14 August 1923

42 Cf. CW 307, *Modern Art of Education*, lecture of 13 and 14 August 1923

43 This approach is also known as the three-stage method, and described in CW 302, *Waldorf Education for Adolescence,* lecture 3, Stuttgart 1921

44 CW 302, *Waldorf Education for Adolescence*, lecture 3, called the 'supplementary course'

45 CW 307, Ilkley, 14 August 1923

46 CW 307, *Modern Art of Education*, lecture 10, Ilkley 14 August 1923

47 *The Foundations of Human Experience*, lecture 13, 4 September 1919

48 *Waldorf Education for Adolescence*, CW 302, lecture 4, Stuttgart 15 June 1921

49 *The Foundations of Human Experience*, CW 293, lecture 11, Stuttgart 2 September 1919

50 Op. cit.

51 *A Social Basis for Education*, CW 192, lecture 4, Stuttgart 11 May 1919

52 CW 300b. Meeting of 6 February 1923
53 Ibid
54 *Waldorf Education for Adolescence*, CW 302, lecture 4,
    Stuttgart 15 June 1921
55 CW 302, lecture 2, 13 June 1921

Christof Wiechert

Teaching –
The Joy of Profession

An Invitation to Enhance Your
(Waldorf) Interest

184 p., Pb., ISBN 978-3-7235-1473-3

To be a teacher and teaching children and youngsters is still a wonderful profession: it never gets dull or boring. But it is also a professional life under pressure. Complex demands, a high profile in professionalism, delivering sound results, yet also being attentive to the individual needs and development of the students and helping parents to understand their own child. All this demands from the teacher a multitasking talent. The teacher is constantly serving others, without time for him- or herself. Working in this profession you can easily loose your balance, the balance between inner needs and demands put on you by children, their performances, the parents and the school organism as a whole. If that happens, then we grow sour in this delightful profession. This book is a guide to find that balance which means gaining access to more energy, more creativity, more joyful responsibility for the sake of healthy students and a healthy profession.

Verlag am Goetheanum